Sep

To

glory!

Priscilla

The Battle
is the Lord's

The Battle
is the Lord's

by Owen C. Carr
with Doug Brendel

Creation House
Carol Stream, Illinois

Back cover photos by Howard Thompson

Published by Creation House, 499 Gundersen Drive, Carol Stream, Illinois 60187

Distributed in Canada: Beacon Distributing Ltd., 104 Consumers Drive, Whitby, Ontario L1N 5T3

Distributed in Australia: Oracle Australia, Ltd., 18-26 Canterbury Road, Heathmont, Victoria 3135

ISBN 0-88419-177-X
Library of Congress Catalog Card No. (applied for)
Printed in the United States of America

Contents

Foreword

What characteristics should you develop in order to become successful?

How can you prepare for a career so that everything you do will lead to ultimate success?

Countless tests have been conducted by innumerable psychologists to provide answers to these questions. Historians and sociologists have added their research and have propounded their theories. To date, however, none has come up with a surefire formula.

The Bible provides a number of interesting suggestions. They are highlighted in the lives of men whom God has used—in both the Old Testament and the New Testament.

Moses, the man who led a band of two million people over a trackless waste of four hundred miles, had the vision of a "promised land." Without visible sources of food or water, providing his own sanitation and transportation for a period of forty years, Moses ultimately brought the complaining, often rebelling, disorganized Children of Israel to the land which God had promised them. The Bible describes Moses as "meek among all men which were on the face of the earth."

David, the second king and by far the greatest in the history of Israel, probably is revered more than any other man in history by Israelis today. He committed adultery with a woman and then had her husband murdered so that she could become his wife. The Bible identifies David as "a man after God's own heart."

In New Testament times the Apostle Paul clearly is the greatest missionary statesman of that day. He probably traveled farther, preached more often and suffered greater persecution for his faith in Jesus Christ than any other man of that day. And ultimately he was killed because of his faith. Yet the Bible describes him as the "chiefest of sinners."

But what does a Kansas farmboy do when he has no education, yet believes God is calling him? What formula will work for him?

The refreshing account that follows is a documentary on spiritual success in our day. No one, including Owen Carr himself, would claim it to be the only formula. It is interesting, however, because it does include elements apparent in the lives of other men whom God has used in other days.

Like the objectives of many pioneers, Carr's vision for Christian television for the Chicago area first appeared so impossible that few could comprehend it.

Wiser heads—especially those sophisticated in the arts of electronic communications—knew the problems. First came the facilities. Then the necessary technicians. Finally the enormous involvements of programing. And overshadowing all was the factor of money, money, money. In fact, more money than most could visualize.

But Owen Carr did not see money as a factor. His vision was for men and women, boys and girls, to be brought into the kingdom of God. And just as secular television with its massive injections of crime, violence and sex were poisoning the minds of millions, he believed that the same technique would be employed to draw many to Jesus Christ.

Yes, this book will reveal Owen Carr's formula for success in overcoming impossible situations. In his case the catalyst was Christian television for the greater Chicago area. Great motivation, to be sure.

But the secret to this motivation is far deeper. What you will find in the pages that follow—difficulties and faith, hardships and more faith, tears and persevering faith, failure and measured success—can come to you as well as to Owen Carr. This, I am sure, is the overwhelming reason why he has given us this account.

Robert Walker, Editor
Christian Life Magazine

Chapter 1

Catastrophe

Tomorrow I'm going to buy a television station.

I will walk into the offices of the Chicago Federation of Labor. A banker will give me a check for $600,000, and I will hand it to the president of the most powerful labor organization in the Midwest. And suddenly—after more than five years of praying and fumbling, making false starts and dreaming foolish dreams—Christians in the greater Chicago area will be able to watch Christian TV programs on Channel 38.

Also by tomorrow night I will be more than $600,000 in debt.

Yes, I had wept and wrestled and prayed for so many months to get a Christian TV station on the air in Chicago that I was primed and ready for all of its consequences—or so I thought.

At the moment, I wanted nothing more than to turn that beautiful check in my hand over to William Lee, the C.F.L.'s president.

And it would happen in the main conference room of the C.F.L. suite in the plush Marina City office building. Tomorrow was the deadline given to us by the Federal Communications Commission (F.C.C.) in Washington, D.C., when they granted us the Channel 38 license two weeks before.

The story had already hit the media: newspapers and television. Newspaper columnists had jeered since the beginning; TV commentators had taken a tongue-in-cheek attitude. But now, tomorrow, the project would finally be completed. Tomorrow at 11 a.m. Channel 38 would be bought from the same C.F.L. leaders who had grinned at me like amused parents when I first told them my plans.

God had led us down a treacherous, nerve-wracking road—but now I could see that this victory had been our destination all along.

Except for one last hairpin curve.

The phone rang at 3:45 that afternoon. I picked it up in the kitchen. It was Martin Ozinga, Jr., our banker at the First National.

He had turned over to his legal department all the paper-work on the loan, he told me. The lawyers had found a problem.

"In our agreement with you," Ozinga said, "you state that you'll have a 'license' from the F.C.C. before we grant you the loan."

"That is correct," I said.

"But the papers you brought back from Washington indicate that you have a 'construction permit' instead of a license."

He was sorry, he said, but the bank couldn't go through with the loan unless we actually had a license.

I had no response. I hung up and felt the warmth drain out of my fingers and into my face. The Chicago Federation of Labor was going to be looking for its money in less than twenty hours.

Where had we gone wrong? What had we missed with the F.C.C.?

My heart began to pound a little faster.

I called our F.C.C. attorney, Morton Berfield, in Washington. He was calm. A 'license' and a 'construction permit' are basically the same, he explained. The F.C.C. always grants a construction permit, then they process all the paperwork and grant the license. Some stations operate five years without a license, Mort told me. It's just a formality.

I could buy that. I hung up and dialed Ozinga back. The phone kept ringing until I looked up at the kitchen clock. It was after 4 p.m.; the bank's switchboard had closed for the weekend.

Tomorrow is the deadline, I said to myself. *Do something.*

I called Bob Honig, one of the bank's vice-presidents who lived in my neighborhood.

He was out, his wife said.

"I must get through to Ozinga," I pleaded. "Maybe he is still at the bank. Do you have a private number for his office? It would probably bypass the switchboard."

"Sorry," she said. "I have no idea—oh, wait. My husband gave me a number years ago. I have never used it. Maybe I can find it. Hold on a minute."

I held on for what seemed like sixty of them.

She came back on the line and read a number. "It's probably not active any longer," she told me. "It's so old. And they have only recently built a large addition to the bank. All the numbers have probably been changed."

I dialed. Ozinga answered.

I passed along what Mort had told me—we had what we needed to operate Channel 38.

Ozinga held fast. The agreement called for a license. We had made the agreement and secured the letter of credit months earlier. But we had no license. He was not going to part with his $600,000. What happens to the money, he wondered out loud, when the federal government refuses to let you on the air for lack of a license?

I argued and wheedled and applied all the psychology I knew. Ozinga would not budge. Slowly I heard the irritation level rising in his voice.

Finally I told him I would work on the problem. Where could he be reached that evening? He would be at his son's home, Ozinga told me reluctantly. It was his son's birthday. I got the message: "Don't call unless you find your license."

The deal with the First National Bank of Evergreen Park had been smooth, deliberate, and cordial. Martin Ozinga, the bank's president and a born-again believer, had looked our operation over and decided we were a safe risk for a let-

11

ter of credit. The credit would help us get the F.C.C. to grant our license. So the bank's only condition for payment of the money, of course, was that we have the F.C.C. license in hand.

A license! "Jerry Rose, our vice-president and general manager, must have the answer," I said to myself.

"Hello, Jerry? Are you standing up or sitting down?"

"Well, uh, I'm standing up. Why?"

"Perhaps you'd better sit down."

I told him what Ozinga had said. Jerry said that it was only a problem of terminology.

"Still," I replied, "he absolutely will not lend us the money until we have a license."

"But that's impossible," Jerry said. "We can't get the license until we get the money. We can't go on the air until we get the money, and we can't get a license until we get on the air."

"I know that, Jerry. But he says he is not going to lend us the money until we get the license."

That evening I called the world's least organized board meeting. The board of directors of Christian Communications of Chicagoland, Inc. gathered at 7 p.m. in The Stone Church in Palos Heights, a suburb of Chicago, where I was pastor. I opened with prayer and then plunged into a description of the problem.

The phone interrupted me. I never answer the phone in any board meeting, but tonight I made an exception. It could be Ozinga calling to report a change of mind.

Instead, I barely recognized the distorted voice I heard. It was my wife, Priscilla, sobbing so violently that I could hardly make out her words. Nicole, our year-and-a-half-old granddaughter in Cincinnati, had developed a fever of more than 104 degrees. She had gone into convulsions and stopped breathing, the result of a virus she had contracted after a severe round of chicken pox. Our daughter Marilyn had administered mouth-to-mouth resuscitation while our six-year-old grandson called his daddy, my son-in-law David, at the church where he was pastor. David called the emergency squad, whose sirens had screamed in to the driveway and then all the way to the hospital. They had no idea what the outcome would be.

Priscilla had been babysitting Nicole when the baby was exposed to the chicken pox, and now an anguished grandma felt responsible for the emergency.

I tried to calm Priscilla over the phone, but she was nearing hysteria. Finally I hung up and dialed Dan and Elaine Wilson. Dan was our outreach minister at The Stone Church, and Elaine was my personal secretary. They were both devoted friends, and I asked them to meet me at the parsonage and then stay with Priscilla after I had left again for the meeting.

The board members sat shocked at the news about the loan failure. It was a crucial hour, nonetheless I excused myself and rushed home. I could do no less.

Priscilla was a shambles. She lay on the bed sobbing uncontrollably.

I held her hand and cried out to God on her behalf. I was powerless to help. Nicole was in God's hands. And I could not get the stalled loan out of my mind.

Within a few moments the Wilsons arrived. Together we prayed with Priscilla for Nicole. The Wilsons stayed. I left.

A silent, deadly conflict burned within me as I walked out the door. My wife of thirty-four years was my most precious and closely guarded treasure—she was the other half of me. Yet now I left her in her deepest crisis.

Television was not Priscilla's burden. She was leery of the whole project and my preoccupation with it. Somehow, vaguely, she had felt trouble coming from the start.

And now—she didn't need this tonight. Another pastor would have left his work behind at a time like this, I told myself. *What kind of priority system do I have, anyway?*

By now it was a pattern. It never failed to grab at my stomach, but I had left Priscilla home alone night after night in pursuit of this dream. I had rarely watched our thirteen-inch black-and-white TV set at all. And yet on so many evenings over the past several years, I had abandoned my wife for TV—the dream of a Christian TV station.

Now I rushed back to the church. As I peered into the night ahead of the car's lights, I sensed that this was only the first episode. I could only dimly see the difficulties which lay ahead for Priscilla and me.

The board had continued the meeting under Vice- Chairman Max Ephraim. They had called Mort Berfield in Washington again, then set up a conference call between Mort, Ozinga, Ozinga's attorney, and us. Over and over again, Ozinga reminded us that he had to act responsibly, that he was personally responsible for the money entrusted to his bank by "widows and orphans."

"He talked so much about the widows and orphans," Mort told me later, "he almost had me in tears!"

Half a dozen other calls also went out that night. For all the talk, for all the repetition, we made no headway whatsoever. Ozinga had dug in to stay.

Nobody had any suggestions on how to get $600,000 in twelve hours.

"The pastor is still smiling," our treasurer, Fred Severance, noted at one point.

"If this weren't God's project," I told him, "I wouldn't be smiling. But since it's His project, He's responsible for it, and I know He's going to work it out."

They were words of faith or foolishness. At the moment, I could not be sure which.

Vaguely I could imagine the meeting with the C.F.L. tomorrow. Twenty-two people representing eight organizations from six states would assemble to watch the banker show up empty-handed.

The half-million-member Chicago Federation of Labor, its president, its treasurer, its board of directors.

Judge Maurice Perlin of the Court of Appeals, a member of the C.F.L. board.

A representative from the multi-million-dollar R.C.A. corporation.

Representatives from the John Hancock Center where the transmitter for Channel 38 was located.

A representative from the Central National Bank.

Anthony LePore, of Ozinga & LePore, representing the First National Bank of Evergreen Park, Illinois.

And Sherman Carmell, of Carmell & Charone, Ltd., representing the Chicago Federation of Labor.

We would be facing—red-faced—this gauntlet of power and prestige.

I stood up at eleven o'clock, having accomplished exactly nothing since Ozinga's call at 3:45 p.m. that afternoon. I shook my head.

"Brethren, we have committed this project to the Lord so many times, let's just commit it to Him once more in prayer. Then let's all go home and get some sleep."

I prayed. It was over.

I looked at the tired board members as they straggled out. "We are fools for Christ's sake," I told myself.

In fact, nothing I had done in five years seemed very wise at the time. God had not given me a traditional game plan, but He had indeed scored some mighty victories in spite of that.

I had played the fool many times before. By now it almost seemed to be a pattern. "What would happen this time?" I wondered.

Chapter 2

Kettle With No Handles

From the day I moved to the Chicago area, the city grabbed me and held me. I was gripped by a burden for the souls of Chicago's seven million people. The church I was pastoring could only account for a fraction of what I felt.

I looked at Chicago and saw a tiny strip of land along Lake Michigan, clogged with the combined populations of Oklahoma, Kansas, Nebraska, and both Dakotas. Here was the heritage of my youth and early ministry that I had expected to spend my life ministering to—a heritage of the plains, transplanted into a single eighty-mile circle. But North Dakota alone, with less than 10 percent of Chicago's population, had more Assemblies of God churches than Chicago and all of her suburbs.

I realized I was living in the midst of a modern metropolitan tragedy, something that could in no way compare to anything I had seen or felt before.

What was God doing to me?

How could one church reach a city so sprawling as Chicago?

Door-to-door visitation was a classic solution. But simple arithmetic told me that the congregation of The Stone Church could knock on a thousand doors a day, seven days a week, fifty-two weeks a year, and not reach all of Chicagoland with the message of God's love—even after twenty years.

So I took a little larger step of faith and considered the possibility of building church buildings. The experts were saying that about half of Chicagoland's seven million people

16

were unchurched. Thinking big (so as not to limit God), I sketched out a plan for one thousand new churches, each seating one thousand—although there had not been half that many thousand-seat churches built in all the years since Chicago became a city in 1837. Total cost of the imaginary project? Your guess. Total time schedule? Dozens of lifetimes. Total impact? Less than one-third of the unchurched population of Chicagoland.

No formula could quench the burning. Any single church was only a drop in the great metropolitan bucket. Millions were yet to be reached. Every trick of the pastoral trade seemed to fold before the colossal need.

I had a monster of a burden and no place to lay it down.

The city's heartbeat became my own.

As weeks slipped by, I began to feel the ebb and flow of the city with more and more sensitivity. Time and time again I found myself weeping over this vast urban mission field.

Perhaps only a farm kid from a simpler life could ache so deeply for such a place as this.

The multitude of cars crawling over the tangled expressways—those cars were no longer traffic; they were souls.

The throngs of pedestrians scurrying past me at stoplights—they were souls.

The long miles of highrises—apartments, offices, warehouses, hotels. Full of souls.

From the air, I saw housetops stretching for endless miles. Tens of hundreds of thousands of souls.

I concealed it within, but the burden bared itself in my sermons nonetheless. Eventually two businessmen in the church invited me to lunch and asked me about it.

"Pastor, you keep saying 'seven million souls,'" one of them scolded, "as if you think we're responsible for all of them."

"We are," I had to tell them. "If we aren't, who will be?"

Before long I found myself speaking openly—over and over—about that responsibility. When we send a missionary to Calcutta, I told the congregation, we don't expect him to

17

reach one little neighborhood. If he doesn't reach the whole city, we feel he's not doing his job. But God placed us in the great Chicago area just as surely as He placed every missionary. And, I emphasized again and again, God expects us to reach our city. If we don't, we're not doing our job either.

But how to do the job? I could preach and pump and promote the concept, but I couldn't put wheels on it. And it continued to sit there.

How?

That question became the haunting refrain of my prayer life.

I began driving the streets of the city, weeping. I walked the aisles of The Stone Church, weeping. I began each day with prayer and Bible study—and weeping.

The immense weight of the burden began to reshape my perception. I saw new truths in my old Bible. Sodom and Gomorrah became a story of God's love for cities—when from childhood I had known it only as a ghastly chronicle of God's wrath. Why had God sent the angels to Abraham with the warning of disaster? My new eyes, bathed in tears of compassion, could see why: Abraham was the only man who knew how to intercede in prayer for his fellow man. He stood alone, overlooking the great double city, and pleaded her case before the Father.

"Will you spare the city for fifty righteous?" he begged. "For forty-five? For forty? For thirty? For twenty? For ten?"

I could feel the blood of Abraham pulsing in my veins. My heart, too, cried out for a city.

I now saw a new story in the book of Jonah. The old story of rebellion and repentance, disaster and deliverance—all of that dimmed against the backdrop of God's great love for the city of Ninevah. Now I saw clearly how God had manipulated even nature itself to get one certain preacher to preach one certain message to save that one certain city.

My new eyes saw the Scriptures recording Jesus weeping only three times—once over a city. It had always been a puzzle to me. Now I could identify with my Lord.

18

My new eyes saw Daniel opening his window three times a day to pray in the direction of Jerusalem. Now, finally, I knew his devotion; and the Chicago skyline became my Jerusalem in times of prayer.

But the old refrain—"How, Lord?"—was the same.

God finally answered the question. It was Saturday, December 19, 1970, a day in history noted for almost nothing,* save the birth of a vision in the family room of our parsonage.

In prayer that morning, the entire burden had swept over me once again, engulfing me like a huge ocean wave. I stood and faced that skyline one more time, and tears began to burn my eyes. Deeply grieved, my heart aching, I stretched out my arms as if to wrap them around Chicagoland itself.

In my mind's eye, I saw Chicago as a huge black kettle, like we used back on the farm in Kansas to make lard in the fall. But the kettle had no handles, and I couldn't get a grip on it. It was too big around.

"How, Lord?" I cried out again. "You love them. You died for them. You've given me this love for them, but you haven't told me *how*."

My passion was spent. My spirit had wrung itself dry. I grew quiet before the Lord.

And then, quietly, as if He were giving friendly advice over lunch, the Holy Spirit spoke to my heart.

"If you had a television station, Owen, it would help."

I blinked and paused. It was a "still, small voice," the prompting of the Holy Spirit, but for the first time in my life it was saying crazy things.

It was almost a laughable suggestion. A television station? I had never even had a television program. My radio ministry consisted of ninety seconds of Bible reading per day.

"If you had a television station, Owen..."

I had considered starting a television ministry at The Stone

---

*Ironically, the *Information Please Almanac* accidentally omitted the entire month of December 1970 from its "News Chronology," almost as if God had called everything of worldwide significance to a standstill in order to plant the seed for Christian television in Chicago.

Church, perhaps thirty minutes a week. But a *station?* Absurd.

"If you had a television station..."

I knew nothing about television other than OFF-ON-VOL. I had no concept whatsoever of the equipment used or the procedures followed.

Even in the deepest recesses of my memory, I could recall only one simple image of television. As TV arrived from the East back in those days, I remembered, the great flat plains of Kansas suddenly sprouted huge towers, strung to the earth with endless strands of cable. I remembered watching the towers going up, with the cords unraveling longer, longer as the towers reached higher into the skies.

But how it all worked was beyond me, even now.

A television station? Ridiculous.

Obviously my own imagination was teasing me. Obviously I had not yet heard from God. I went back to my praying.

"How, Lord? How?"

But the words were hollow. The old refrain didn't sing the same. I gave up on praying after a while that morning. I was too distracted by that crazy idea about a television station. Instead, I turned to the Bible—something certainly more trustworthy than my own intellect at this point.

The day before, I had stopped at the end of Isaiah 53. Today I picked up at Isaiah 54.

The second verse reached out from the page and shook me.

"Enlarge the place of thy tent, and let them stretch forth the curtains of thine habitations; spare not, *lengthen thy cords,* and strengthen thy stakes."

I stared at the page, astonished, seeing once again those huge television towers going up across the horizons of my past. Surely this was coincidence.

"For thou shalt break forth," the next verse continued, "on the right hand and on the left...

"Fear not," the fourth verse declared, "for thou shalt not be ashamed: Neither be thou confounded, for thou shalt not be put to shame..."

Amazed, I read through the chapter, with verse after verse

popping out directly into my field of vision. Some had that ominous look of the future, which I couldn't even identify at the time: "No weapon that is formed against thee shall prosper," verse seventeen promised, "and every tongue that shall rise against thee in judgment thou shalt condemn..." I had no idea as I sat in my cozy parsonage that enemies would soon rise up against me both inside and outside the body of believers.

As my thoughts fell together in a jumble of questions and objections, my eye fell upon verse eight of the following chapter: "For my thoughts are not your thoughts, neither are your ways my ways, saith the Lord: For as the heavens are higher than the earth, so are my ways higher than your ways, and my thoughts than your thoughts."

I stopped. I read the verse again. Then I read it again. And yet again.

Then I laid my hand on the page and said, "Lord, if You're thinking what I *think* You're thinking, then Your thoughts are certainly *not* my thoughts."

But, as if to reassure me that He was indeed speaking His will to me clearly, the Holy Spirit pointed me to verses ten and eleven: "For as the rain cometh down, and the snow from heaven, and returneth not thither, but watereth the earth, and maketh it bring forth and bud, that it may give seed to the sower, and bread to the eater: so shall my Word be that goeth forth out of my mouth.

"It shall not return unto me void, but it shall accomplish that which I please, and it shall prosper in the thing whereto I sent it."

My eyes raced ahead, barely able to absorb the kaleidoscope of confirming words. Finally I came to rest at Isaiah 58:1: "Cry aloud, spare not, lift up thy voice like a trumpet, and show my people..."

I closed my Bible and sat in awe.

I was shaken. Although I could not understand what had happened, this vivid experience was unforgettable. The choice words of Isaiah were indelibly branded on my heart, to be recalled again and again in the weeks and months to come.

For some unknowable reason, God had prepared me for this strange thing. My credentials were worthless. I was perhaps less likely to succeed than any of my fellow pastors in Chicago. But God was not speculating in the natural. In the natural I was no better a risk than Moses, who knew nothing about turning rods into serpents or serpents into rods or water into blood or dust into lice or the Red Sea into a freeway. Moses only knew God, and on that basis God received all the glory for everything Moses did.

And the only worthwhile credential I had was that I knew the same God Moses knew—and had communed with Him daily for years. Apparently God had taken this single credential—if it could even be called that—and spun it into a frightening, wonderful, impossible job description—for a job I neither needed nor deserved. Nor wanted, for that matter.

I had read Mark 11:24 dozens of times: "What things soever ye desire, when you pray, believe that ye receive them, and ye shall have them." I had always put the emphasis on *desire* in that verse. Now I saw that the emphasis really belongs on *when you pray*. Mine was a burden born in prayer—a desire to reach Chicago, born in prayer. It was a burden completely alien to me, but one that God had decided to house within my heart. In the coming years, I would rely again and again on that principle: "Lord, this whole thing is Yours."

Days stretched into weeks and then months. In every spare moment, I found myself praying about the concept—such as it was, with no name or description or timetable attached.

In all those months of prayer and perplexity, I only tested the idea on two people. The first test came only a few days after the initial encounter with God. I was sitting in my office at the church toying with the idea. On a whim, I called in my secretary, Linda Schmidgall, a close and trusted friend, who had worked for me in two churches. As she sat in my office, I told her about my burden for Chicago and where the Lord had brought me with it.

Linda responded. In a matter of minutes she had formed a bandwagon of one. From that moment forward, she became the strongest single rooter I had. Linda existed in a continuum of enthusiasm. She never lost the high hopes that sprang up in her heart during that first whimsical conversation in my office.

The only other tryout I gave the concept was at home. It was quite a long time after I shared the idea with Linda. The idea was working me over once again; my mind was filled with glimmering possibilities. One day I said to Priscilla, "Let me tell you about this new idea I've got."

She looked at me sharply. She knew the tone of voice. She was the realist of our team.

"Don't," she replied coolly. "I don't want to throw a wet blanket on it."

It wasn't until months later that I finally risked it anyway. Priscilla's first reaction was almost identical to mine: "What would you want with a television station? You *never* watch TV!"

It was a good question. I had no answer for her.

Coca-Cola finally convinced me God could be right. Coca-Cola does not build large buildings, and then try to lure people into them for a drink of their product. Instead they build a distribution center and take their product to where the people are. Availability is salability.

Television is where America shops. She fills her mind full of it every day. She buys what television sells.

Like Coca-Cola, God wanted His product on Chicago's market. And that—finally—I could understand.

There was only one problem left—and that sad old refrain: "How, Lord?"

Chapter 3

Little Red Engine

God would not let go of me. He began bombarding me with "go" signals.

We began the New Year of 1971 at The Stone Church by setting aside a "Week of Faith and Victory." Each evening I asked a different deacon or elder to speak, beginning on January 4 with George Decker.

Then the night Decker spoke, he picked up on the tent theme and ran with it. He spun it out into a major challenge—to "enlarge, lengthen, and strengthen the tent"—and then told the congregation point-blank, "I believe we can do it."

He had no idea what he was saying to me.

But let's be practical, I protested to the Lord. *It takes a bundle of money to produce television.*

Less than a week later, on a Sunday morning at five-thirty, I was praying in my home about the money monster—and how to overcome it. As I opened my Bible, the Holy Spirit pressed two verses of Scripture into my mind:

"The earth is the Lord's, and the fulness thereof, the world and they that dwell therein" (Psalms 24:1).

"Thou shalt remember the Lord thy God: for it is he that giveth thee power to get wealth" (Deuteronomy 8:18).

George Decker is right, the Lord said to me. *You can do it. How much more direct can my Word be?*

As spring approached, The Stone Church hired an assistant pastor, Vern McNally. Vern had just moved to Chicago when I found myself chatting with him about the area's huge population.

"There must be some way," I said, "to reach this mass of people."

Vern had no idea of my thinking, but he responded quickly. "We'll have to use TV," he said without blinking.

And God quietly said to me again, *You can do it.*

Two days later, I assembled the staff of The Stone Church. For the first time I shared with them the dream of using television to reach the Chicago area with the Gospel. They were delighted and they pledged themselves to pray about it.

None of us, however, had any idea how to proceed.

As spring bloomed full into summer, I attended a denominational camp meeting in Carlinville, Illinois. On Friday night, July 2, I was praying at the altar when George Mandel, one of the leaders of the denomination in Illinois, suddenly laid both his hands on me. He began to pray that God would help me give witness of Jesus Christ *"to every house* in Chicagoland."

Another nudge. It seemed as if God was saying over and over, *you can do it.* Systematically He was convincing me that the impossible was indeed possible. Almost like the little red engine, I was being coached to huff and puff *"I think I can, I think I can"* until the notion became action.

Day after day I prayed and wept. Day after day the immense burden grew heavier. I ached for a way to put wheels on the vision. But no wheels appeared.

Then early in 1972, I walked into a conference room at the Holiday Inn in Joliet, Illinois. A statewide ministers' meeting was scheduled. I had never met Ossie B. Jones, a popular evangelist, but I had heard his name many times. When he was introduced to the group I finally connected a face to the name.

At one point in the meeting we paused to pray for one another one-on-one. I clasped hands with a minister near me, and we prayed together briefly.

As I turned around, I saw Ossie Jones coming across the room in my general direction. He was headed past me, but he put out his hand for a quick handshake. As I took his hand, he suddenly stopped, threw his other arm around me, and began praying fervently.

"Lord, You have laid on this man's heart a vision," he began, "and it scares him to death."

My senses began to tingle.

"He does not know what to do with what You have given him," Jones continued. "He does not know where to turn. He does not know whom to talk to."

My mind was reeling as I sensed the presence of the Holy Spirit.

"But You are faithful, Lord," Jones prayed. "You will direct his life. You will bring to him the people he needs to know. You will cause him to meet the people who will help him."

He stopped abruptly, and walked on.

I stood transfixed.

So this was not some far-fetched man-made scheme after all, I reasoned. It was a genuine move of God, directing my life, laying a course for me. It was a God-given vision, and He would put the wheels in motion Himself.

In the meantime I would do all I could. I would keep on praying, keep on searching the Scriptures, keep on weeping over the city of Chicago.

On March 21, 1971, in a moment, as if someone had flipped a switch inside me, I knew it was time. I had been fasting and now was praying in the sanctuary. Suddenly I knew it was time to see the board of The Stone Church. Time to put the wheels in motion.

"This...could well be the most significant meeting, of any kind, ever held in the Chicago area, including political conventions, corporate amalgamations, and gatherings, large and small."

Thus I began my strident summons to the nine deacons and six staffers assembled—a little ironically—in the junior high Sunday School department of the church.

"...What happens here tonight could do more to affect the lives of the teeming millions in the Chicago area than anything that has ever been done since this city was founded."

It was a sweeping concept, certainly a grandiose generalization. But I feel just as strongly today that what I verbalized that evening is still the truth. As I besieged my little group of listeners, the statistics alone bore out the staggering potential of our project.

Ninety-five percent of all American homes had at least one television set at that time, and the percentage was climbing rapidly.

Elementary students were viewing an average of twenty hours of television every week during the school year alone.*

The typical American high schooler was being graduated with 15,000 hours of television having passed through his system, over 4,000 hours more than he had spent in school.[+] That was also almost 12,000 hours more than he had spent in church—that is, if he attended Sunday School, morning and evening worship, youth meeting, and midweek service every week for twelve years.

The average high school graduate had also seen over 500 feature movies that year. Over half of all weekly moviegoers were between ten and nineteen years old at the time. Two-thirds were between fifteen and twenty-five. Both figures have climbed since then.

Then I talked to the board and the staff about the viewer himself. Statisticians tell us that we learn 6 percent of what we know through taste, touch, and smell combined. Another 11 percent is learned through hearing. But what we see teaches us 83 percent of everything we know.

Then, on our capacity to remember: we recall 10 percent of what we read, 20 percent of what we hear, 30 percent of what we see. But when we both see and hear, we retain a full 50 percent.

If we could picture the coverage of a television station, I told the group, as the canvas of a tent, the canvas would

---

*According to Dr. Paul Witley of Northwestern University.
[+] According to Father John Culkin of Fordham University.

27

reach out from the towers on the John Hancock Building in a radius of eighty miles—encompassing a potential audience of more than eight million souls.

The statistics went on and on: chronicles of apathy among Americans about religion, of the weakness of evangelistic efforts after a prospect leaves college, of powerful media ministries in other states and other countries.

But the bottom line—no surprise—was money. The CBS affiliate in Chicago, WBBM-TV 2, wanted $3,600 per half-hour of prime time for local coverage only. To produce a thirty-minute weekly program would cost over $187,000 a year in air time alone—to say nothing of program cost which more than doubles the figure.

"But there is another way," I hastened to point out, "possibly less expensive, certainly more effective...to have our own television station."

I had no concrete suggestions to offer.

"Since we don't have any money," I offered boldly, "and since we are going to have to believe God for even a little, it won't be any harder to believe Him for a lot."

I had no idea where to start, except to call the F.C.C. in Washington to see if any channels were available in Chicago.

I did ask the board to send me and another board member on a fact-finding trip to see other television ministries in operation. I wanted Richard Weidmann to go with me, but I didn't mention his name. Other than that, I was open. Wide open.

I looked at the board. The board looked at me. They sat there and sat there. No claps of thunder. No flashes of light. No sound.

After an interminable silence, Howard Dexheimer leaned back and asked the key question: "Well, Pastor, how much could this cost?"

I had to tell him the truth.

"I don't know," I responded, looking him squarely in the eye. "Maybe ten million dollars."

A few eyebrows went up.

"But even if we try and fail," I told them, "I believe we

can be forgiven. If we don't try, though, will God forgive us? Will we forgive ourselves?

"There are eight million people within our grasp," I went on, "and we must make an attempt to reach them."

The only concrete suggestion I had made, the fact-finding trip, was now called into question. To phone the key people at each of those ministries, some of the deacons felt, would be just as worthwhile as traveling all over the country and spending all that money.

Oddly, it was Richard Weidmann who spoke up in defense.

"No, this kind of thing has to be done in person," he said, although he didn't know I was going to ask him to accompany me. "You can't absorb this kind of thing over the phone."

The board voted $1,200 for a fact-finding trip. It was the first earthly green light the vision had received.

Church duties pressed in on me. Scheduling stops at all of the ministries in one trip proved difficult. Delays and changes. Postponements. Cancellations.

It was eight months later, a chilly February day, when I finally left the ground at O'Hare International Airport.

In place after place, in eleven churches in three states, Dick and I saw the future of our own work unfolding before us. It was not entirely a pleasant feeling. At one point Dick just looked at me with tears filling his eyes and said, "It makes me feel like we aren't doing anything."

The operations Dick and I visited were varied. They had different means, different ends. But there was one unifying thread, one factor that surfaced in every city we visited, a factor that made each ministry kin to the next: every ministry had been conceived by the spark of enthusiasm in a local church, igniting a long-incubated dream nested in one person's heart.

So the formula was right. Perhaps the odds for success were longer in our case, with Chicago ranking second only to New York City among the biggest and tightest television markets. Ours would be a tougher metropolitan nut to crack perhaps, at least in the natural.

But God had obviously worked before in other cities. Now the great question came into clear focus: could His formula also work in Chicago?

Chapter 4

Faith Plus Energy Equals Foolishness

Dad looked at me hard when I told him I was going to be a preacher. He was a Kansas farmer. He had the feeling that anybody who didn't farm didn't really work for a living.

He had two daughters, but I was his only son, less than three months married, and as a butcher already making more money than he.

Hours later, Dad finally responded to the announcement.

"So you're gonna be a preacher, huh?" he said.

"Yes, I believe that is what God wants me to do," I replied.

"Then all I've got to say," Dad said, "is, if you're going to start, then don't ever stop! And if you're going to stop, then don't ever start!"

He meant it when he said that was all he had to say. I spent twenty years in the ministry before he died, and he never again mentioned it. He heard me preach many times, but he never commented on the sermons. Occasionally, through third parties, I heard that my father was proud of me.

My mother had quietly nurtured me in the fear of the Lord from the day I was born in a three-room house in Okmulgee, Oklahoma. Perhaps she made it inevitable that I would become a minister, for she taught me carefully and consistently to love the Lord. I accepted Christ as an eleven-year-old in a revival crusade at Kaw City, Oklahoma near the close of the great depression. From then on, my mother's faithful seed-sowing continued to reap a flourishing harvest in my life. I walked behind the horse-drawn plow, talking to the Lord. I rode Dad's six-disc weeder up and down the rows of corn, praising God and telling Jesus how much I wanted to be like Him. I drove the tractor through the fields, singing His praises. A hunger to know God—instilled by my mother—began to grow within me.

But a lifetime of ministry never crossed my mind. I would have dismissed it if it had. How silly a notion.

Then I met a man who revolutionized my life. I was a high school senior, cutting meat for a frozen foods plant, when he walked in with my pastor. He was introduced as V.G. Greisen, a church leader in Kansas. He had a funny accent. The two men made their purchase and left.

But the next time I saw V.G. Greisen, his eyes lit up, and he bellowed out my name. He had not forgotten me. It was the beginning of a lifelong friendship.

Greisen had a fascination for young people and children, and they likewise for him. Often when he visited a family he spent the entire time playing with the children of the home.

"Adults always know how to behave when somebody comes," he explained to me years later. "But children are themselves. When I know what the children are, I know what the parents are."

But this was only a sliver of what V.G. Greisen knew about human nature. I have never met a person who so consistently and accurately read the hearts of men. As he filled positions of leadership among ministers around the world, he invariably knew when to encourage and when to deflate the various egos in his care.

It was Greisen's life-example that shaped my entire ministry. He believed in two universal forces: faith and energy.

Greisen lived in a continuum of energy. As a young man he had been known to roll up his sleeves and walk across a flooded street on his hands!

He had sailed from his native Denmark in 1909, disembarking in New York City with no knowledge whatsoever of the English language. He had a dollar and a half in his pocket, although he had no idea how much that might buy. He taught himself to speak English and to type at seventy words a minute using only four fingers.

He began to preach in his thick Danish accent, and soon the power of his personality and the power of the Holy Spirit in his life propelled him into places of authority.

Greisen never had enough work to do. Without a secretary he wrote thousands of letters to people all over the world. He carried postcards in his pocket. In church services, while some one else made the announcements, Greisen wrote cards to discouraged preachers or children he had met in his travels.

At the age of sixty-five, Greisen accepted a job overseeing all his denomination's missionary work in Europe, the Middle East, and southern Asia. He served with distinction for four years. Then in his seventieth year, he wrote me a letter:

"I am getting out of this office. Jesus said the field is the world, and they have limited me to Europe, the Middle East, and South Asia. I must get into the field."

When he was nearly eighty, Greisen and youngsters still had that old mutual fascination. By now he was laughing with a whole new generation of children, but he was laughing just the same. He had barely slowed down at all.

When I became pastor at The Stone Church, I wanted him to come and speak. During the service he suddenly decided to sing. I was amazed: he sang a song I had heard him sing decades before, but his voice was still the same—the strong, clear voice of a fifty-year-old tenor.

He was energy personified for over eighty years. When finally infirmity beset him, he still felt the Church had moved too slowly in those eighty years toward fulfilling the Great Commission.

"I may have to live to 120," he chuckled. "Not that I want to," he added, "but the need is there."

And yet energy was only half of V.G. Greisen's trademark.

The other half, unshakable faith, was an even more powerful force that had its effect on me.

"If you're sick, trust God for your healing," he often said. "And if you die, don't believe it."

One day during his term in Europe, Greisen was traveling across the continent by car with missionary Richard Dortch. Without warning, Greisen was struck with excruciating pain. He pitched and rolled in the back seat, groaning and calling out to God in prayer.

"He had suffered as long as I could stand it," Dortch told me later. "So I said, 'Do you want me to stop and call ahead for a doctor?'"

Suddenly Greisen stopped groaning and sat up with a quizzical look on his face.

"Why?" he asked Dortch. "Are you sick?"

Moments later Greisen was smiling, "There. That's the end of it," he said triumphantly. "God has healed me."

Greisen's faith gave him an unusual holy boldness. When he visited his native Denmark at the close of World War II, he determined to build a Bible school in the country to help strengthen the churches there. He chose a young man to head the school, and then set about to secure a car for him. At the time it was illegal for ministers outside the state church to own cars.

Back in America, Greisen wrote to the King of Denmark asking for special permission. He got a reply—negative—from one of the King's subordinates.

Greisen was indignant. He wrote the underling, stating that he had written to the King, not to some staff members, and he expected his letter to be brought directly to the King's attention.

He signed the letter "Bishop V.G. Greisen."*

---

*The title stuck. From then on, Greisen was known in ministerial circles as the Bishop. It was a justified title. Titus 1:7-9 says, "For a bishop must be blameless, as the steward of God . . . a lover of hospitality, a lover of good men, sober, just, holy, temperate; Holding fast the faithful word as he hath been taught, that he may be able by sound doctrine both to exhort and to convince the gain-sayers."

Before long the self-appointed "Bishop" got word that the King of Denmark had granted special permission for the new school's director to have a car. +

It was this faith, this energy that became my model for ministry. No matter that the formula sometimes produced what looked like foolishness. Greisen looked foolish in the eyes of men about half the time, and yet it was clear that here was a true man of God.

I could aspire to that, I decided. It was within my grasp. I might preach poorly and sing worse, but I could fill my ministry with faith and energy.

And, if neccessary, the inevitable foolishness.

I went to Greisen with my decision to preach. At the time he headed the work of the denomination in the state of Kansas. I did not know that married people went to Bible school. I asked him to find me a church.

He must have curbed the urge to laugh. I had never spoken in public, could not sing or play an instrument, had no knowledge of the ministry. No one in my family was a minister.

Indeed, I had struggled with these facts for two weeks, around the clock since the moment God had spoken to me. I had lain awake nights, searching for God's reason for calling me, of all people. I wasn't resisting, but I had to be sure. And finally, standing at the meat block, I stopped my work and talked to God in the simplest way:

"I don't understand this. But somehow I feel You are calling me to preach. If this is so, then here I am. I may make a

---

+ Greisen's letters have a history of their own. Years later, with the school well under way, one of the teachers began circulating rumors that the school was going broke. Greisen, furious, fired off a letter to the faculty: "Nations may rise and fall, but that school will go on. Kings and rulers may rise and fall, but that school will go on. Businesses may fail, but that school will go on. Hell may freeze over, but that school will go on, because that school is a part of the Church, and Jesus said, 'The gates of hell shall not prevail against my Church'!"

fool of myself trying, but if this is Your will for me then I will try."

Immediately the struggle ended. I had quit my job, and now I stood before Greisen, asking for a church to lead.

Two churches were looking for pastors at the moment, he said. One was in a town of 200, with an attendance of thirty or forty. The other was in a town of twenty-five, with an attendance of one family and some neighborhood kids— thirteen in all.

"Vell, let me see," Greisen said in his Danish way. "Vhat vould I do, if I vere you, but know vhat I know?"

He sat back and pondered it a moment.

"I tink I vould go to Gerlane."

It was the smaller church. From my vantage point thirty-five years later, I see what he meant by "knowing vhat I know." In this little church I couldn't possibly hurt anybody. These people had served God so long that they would serve God with or without a pastor. He was sending me where I could do the least damage.

Priscilla, my bride of a few weeks, and I slid into the seat of our 1933 Chevy Coupe, squeezed together and drew a chalk line on the seat to show how much room we took up. Then we began loading our belongings around that space. We filled the floor, the seats, the trunk; we tied things to the fenders and the running boards.

It was 1942; war was on. Gasoline was rationed. Gerlane was 120 miles west.

"I'll never see my mother again," she said as we drove away.

It was the only time a transition would upset her—until Channel 38 came into our lives.

Chapter 5

Crossroads

Our first church and parsonage were the end of the line—literally. They sat side by side at the end of a dirt road. The railroad track also ended at our yard.

Weeds had overgrown the house during its long months of vacancy. As we pulled up in front, all we could see was the roof of the parsonage. The outhouse had completely disappeared.

Our water supply came from a bucket lowered into a cistern. Several dead mice and hundreds of insects floated on the water's surface.

The church was lighted by four Coleman lamps suspended at strategic points. Part of the pastor's responsibility was to pump up these gas lamps and light them before each evening service. In the year we spent at Gerlane, we never got through an entire service with all four lamps lit.

The one family in the church, Mr. and Mrs. Arthur Colborn, were faithful saints. Both parents, four of their five children, and Grandma Colborn attended every service.

My salary was five dollars per week plus all the eggs the Colborns' hens could lay on Sunday. At first this meant one or two dozen eggs would come our way each week. But as the hens grew more productive we began getting up to a hundred eggs a week. Priscilla bravely experimented with them and found plenty of different ways to prepare them. Even so, eventually we had eaten all the eggs we could endure.

Potatoes were our other staple. We ate them all the usual ways, and a few unusual ways. Finally one night I sat down to dinner and found a large bowl of fried potatoes standing alone on the table.

I looked at the potatoes, then at my bride of less than a year.

"Honey, I can't eat another potato."

"You don't love me anymore," she sniffed, "or you would eat what I fix." (Kindly, she did not remind me that she was fixing all I was providing.)

After the tears, of course, she did not feel like eating. To prove my love for her, I ate all the potatoes myself.

Before long I began hunting for a part-time job. As a meat-cutter who had failed his father at farming, I had no business working on a farm. But I found that farmers would pay up to twenty cents an hour for a ten- or twelve-hour day. It was too good to pass up.

Soon we were buying a little meat once in a while.

The long hours taught me a truth about my career: the ministry is basically work. The glamor was not real.

No church deserves a pastor as dumb as I was. I never recommend that anyone go into the ministry without college training.

How could I hope to grow as a minister of the Gospel when I did not even know how to pastor a single family?

One day I shared some amazing information with the Heavenly Father. "Lord, these people have served You longer than I have lived," I said. "What can I tell them that they don't already know?"

He answered quietly, in the same "still, small voice" that had called me into His service.

"They don't have to answer in eternity for your sermon outlines," the voice prompted. "But they will have to answer for what my Word says. So don't worry about the sermon outlines. Just give them my Word."

That simple encounter with God plunged me into a search of the Scriptures that still goes on today. I began to get up at five o'clock every morning to read my Bible and pray. The thin-walled house was frigid on winter mornings, but I stoked the stove and wrapped myself in quilts and studied and talked with the Lord.

Ignorant as I was, I had no idea where to begin except at

the beginning. I began at Genesis 1:1 and proceeded to read the Bible through.

What an adventure! I discovered things in the Word that I had never heard mentioned in church. Like a wide-eyed child at Disneyland, I took in the Scriptures story by story, chapter by chapter, with astonishment and delight.

That childlike delight still floods my mind and heart as I read, although by now I have gone through the Book forty times. And the sense of appreciation grows.

I did not spend those early morning hours hunting sermons. I had no idea how to construct one anyway.

But I prayed, "God, make me a preacher of Your Word. Help me lay aside my own ideas and declare Your truths to the people."* And God illuminated His Word each week. I never went to a service without something to share directly from the Lord.

Every sermon was abundant with Scripture, read directly from the Book itself, a practice God never let me quit. Trends have come and gone, and at times my Scripture-centered sermons have seemed primitive in comparison to others. But the Heavenly Father has always reminded me of the first ministerial training He gave me: *"Just give them My Word."*

It soon became obvious why God had called me into the ministry. There were dozens of tiny farm towns in western Kansas. I was going to move from one community to the next over the space of the next twenty-five years and enjoy what I believed would be an immensely satisfying ministry among the people of my own heritage.

I could not provide live entertainment from the pulpit. I lacked the magnetism of the high-profile preachers. I lacked the expertise of an administrator.

---

*God faithfully answered my prayer. Twenty years later the president of a Bible college introduced me to the student body. "We are always happy to welcome Owen Carr to the pulpit of this college," he said, "because when we do, we bring to you students a man who is a preacher of God's Word." I got up to speak, but getting started was difficult. There was a big lump in my throat.

Mine was to be simply a ministry of the Word, a ministry of building faith in the hearts of the people. It was all I knew.

I began to see the elements of V.G. Greisen's life-pattern emerging in my work. Faith and energy were producing a consistent ministry. I still played the fool in dozens of ways—it was an inevitable byproduct of the formula. But I soon discovered the ultimate result of the formula: faith plus energy equals *faithfulness*.

And this faithfulness, I realized—the product of faith plus energy—was to be the single cornerstone of my entire ministry.

"God, make me faithful," I prayed earnestly every morning. "I can't do what others have done, but help me to be faithful. I may not have ability, but help me to be faithful."

No crowds would flock to hear my oratory. No throngs would pack an auditorium to watch this carrot-topped preacher. In fact, I was terrified when some close friends of ours, Glen and Ann Ahlf, offered to recommend me for their church in Medicine Lodge, the county seat, with a population of 2000. The church averaged forty-five people.

"You'll never get me into a big church!" I vowed to them.

But it happened anyway. In the summer of 1943, Priscilla and I packed up our new baby boy and moved to Corwin. It was a much bigger city: population seventy-five, church membership twenty-three.

After more than a year there, V.G. Greisen called me and asked me to take a church in Pomona, Kansas. We moved again. God was obviously fulfilling my plan for my ministry—pastoring in small towns.

It was in Pomona (population 500), that my ho-hum ministry stopped yawning and began to stretch. A light began to dawn in my early-morning prayer times. One morning two passages that (ironically) I had known all my life suddenly meshed together in my heart: "God is no respecter of persons: But in every nation he that feareth him, and worketh righteousness, is accepted with him" (Acts 10:34,35) and "Jesus Christ the same yesterday, and today, and forever" (Hebrews 13:8).

My mind raced through the biblical Hall of Fame—to Abraham, Isaac, Jacob, Joseph, Saul, David, Solomon, Daniel, the three Hebrew children—then into the New Testament, to Peter, James, John, and Paul.

They were greats.

But God is no respecter of persons, I cried within myself. *And Jesus Christ is the same today as He was then.*

Then God would do for me what he had done for these! God could bless my ministry just as much as He blessed theirs!

The mantle of fear, of timidity, began to shake itself off me that day. I might be only a two-bit preacher in a small town, nevertheless I took hold of the Scriptures and laid claim to their promises from that day forward.

Suddenly prayers were answered miraculously; sinners accepted Christ, sick people were healed. Week after week the drama unfolded as the Holy Spirit swept through our little church.

I was beginning to learn a life-changing spiritual principle: God does not require education; He does not even require ability. But He does require submission, obedience, faithfulness.

My fledgling ministry was on the move.

Before two years were up, Greisen called again, this time with a tougher assignment. A small, discouraged church in Iola, Kansas, needed a pastor. It had grown for a time, but now the church had shrunk to fewer than twenty people. They were thinking of closing the church.

We brought two children with us this time. David now had a little sister, Marilyn, born during our term at Pomona.

I had to sell our car because I had no money for payments. I began walking all over the town of Iola, with its 7,500 people. I called on parishioners and prospects, packed groceries on my shoulder, and covered the five blocks between home and church, all on foot.

I began to set aside each Friday as a day of prayer and fasting. The congregation slowly expanded. Finally I had to have a car to cover the growing territory. I bought an old junker with a cloth top and holes in the floor.

Money was scarce for our growing family. Again I looked for work.

Back to the farms, this time selling electrical farming equipment. Late each night I loaded the old car with equipment, then caught the farmers each morning, buckets in hand, just as they came out for milking. By the time Iola woke up, I was back in town going about the business of pastoring the church.

For five months no one in the church knew I was moonlighting to feed my children.

The church grew in number, in spirit, in strength. I shocked them on a Sunday morning by telling them what I had been doing, but now I was stepping out in faith and quitting my job to devote full time to the church.

The people rallied beautifully. Spurred on by faith, the complexion of the congregation changed. The Iola people no longer moped and talked about disbanding. God was at work because of a little faith and continuing faithfulness.

Months later, I was driving V.G. Greisen across the state for meetings. He began to review my early ministry as we rode together.

"Carr, the thing that has characterized your ministry," he began, "is faithfulness. When I sent you to Gerlane, there wasn't much there. But you were faithful. When you pastored in Corwin, there wasn't much there. But you were faithful. We sent you to Pomona. Again you were faithful.

"Then we asked you to go to Iola. That was a very difficult place. The people were discouraged. But you were faithful."

I grinned as I drove. God had truly answered that persistent prayer.

At every stop, I learned new lessons. It was Iola, Kansas, that taught me to pray. God honored my Friday fasts. He also sent Moses and Ruth Copeland to us for two weeks of services.

Moses Copeland was one of the great prayer warriors. Each morning, he and I met at the church at seven. First he

42

prayed for me, then he asked me to pray for him. Finally we prayed together. In two weeks he taught me a lifetime of prayer principles.

It was a divine concoction: large and equal amounts of God's Word and prayer. No ministry could fail to fulfill God's purpose if the pastor, along with the people, ingested it.

I didn't realize it as the Copelands drove away, but God had just entrusted that perfect potion into my hands, and He intended me to drink deeply of it.

God moved us again and again, teaching us, molding us, using us. For two years we pastored in Lyons, Kansas, where the young congregation built a new parsonage and started a sanctuary. For five years I directed youth activities for Kansas churches from a state office in Wichita. This post took me into adjacent states for ministry. For the first time, Owen Carr and the rest of the world got a glimpse of each other.

Eventually I came to the Edwards Street Assembly in Alton, Illinois, just north of St. Louis. Here God grabbed me, after nearly twenty-five years in the ministry, and drew me into a startling new direction.

Edwards Street was a good church, a solid church, full of wonderful people who enjoyed meeting together. But sinners were not coming to Christ.

I was still praying and reading the Word every morning at five o'clock but before long I began to yearn for revival, and my prayers grew more intense.

Nothing happened.

Acts 6:4 jumped out at me one morning as I was reading. "We will give ourselves continually to prayer," it said, "and to the ministry of the word."

Immediately I knew I held the answer in my hands. God wanted me to translate "faith plus energy" into consistent action in my everyday life. And that consistent action was to be the "large and equal amounts of God's Word and prayer" that Moses Copeland had demonstrated for me. Between these two great men of God, Greisen and Copeland, I found the power source for the Christian walk.

I opened my appointment calendar and began marking off blocks of time for prayer, three hours every day. Some fell at every part of the day, from early morning to deep in the night. I was determined to turn "faith plus energy" into a working principle in my life and ministry.

I told no one.

The long hours of prayer and reading were not all hours of exultation. Some were refreshing, but many hours simply became sessions of discipline.

Each week I waited anxiously to sense a change in the services.

Nothing happened.

Day after day I prayed, for an entire month.

Still nothing happened.

I prayed every day of the second month.

Likewise.

I prayed every day of the third month.

There was no change whatsoever.

One evening after a board meeting, one of the deacons went home and awakened his wife.

"We have to pray for the pastor," he told her with alarm. "I have a feeling if people don't start getting saved, our pastor is going to die."

The pressure was leaking.

On a Saturday morning I went to the sanctuary before six, hungry to see God move. I began to pray by quoting Jeremiah 33:3: "Call unto me, and I will answer thee, and show thee great and mighty things, which thou knowest not."

Suddenly it dawned on me that I didn't know anything else from Jeremiah 33. I looked it up and began to read. The Lord spoke to me in verses ten and eleven: "Thus saith the Lord; again there shall be heard in this place . . . the voice of joy, the voice of gladness, the voice of the bridegroom, the voice of the bride, and the voice of them that shall say, Praise the Lord of hosts . . ."

I got up early the next morning to put the final touches on my Sunday morning message. In a moment the sermon withered from my mind and Jeremiah 33 sprang up in full bloom in its place.

That morning I preached that revival was coming. God wanted to send it, if only His people would call on His name.

People prayed well past noon. Souls began finding Christ in our services. Revival swept Edwards Street, and those years became some of the most thrilling of my entire ministry.

Never one to throw away a good thing, I continued to block off those three hours a day.

One day about that time I was thinking back over the twenty-five years of ministry. How could it happen to a timid country boy with virtually no education? Plainly, there was only one answer: the early morning vigils of thousands of hours of prayer and Bible study claiming souls for the Lord, healings for bodies and renewal for believers had paid off. I made a decision. If that formula could bring someone as unlikely as Owen Carr to this place in the Body of Christ, then I would bank the rest of my life's work on the same: large and equal amounts of God's Word and prayer.

God took note of that decision. But little did I realize how much would be needed in the days ahead.

Chapter 6

Family Joke

We were still in Corwin, Kansas, when one day V.G. Greisen came for lunch. He was giving me some wise advice over the kitchen table and a cup of coffee.

"If you're ever asked to preach at the First Assembly in Wichita," he told me, "be sure to go. Someday they may be looking for a pastor. They might remember you."

"Oh no," Priscilla cut in, with a sly grin, "he doesn't intend to go to Wichita. Owen's going to pastor The Stone Church in Chicago!"

Greisen broke up into his infectious laugh. Then all three of us laughed. It was a pretty funny line, considering who I was and what The Stone Church was.

The Stone Church stood grand and tall as one of the great and venerable churches of Chicago and, in fact, the nation. Woodrow Wilson was still President when The Stone Church became a cornerstone of the new fellowship of churches known as the Assemblies of God.

The greatest gospel preachers kept her waiting list filled as they stood in line for a chance to speak from her pulpit. The Stone Church was also a giant among missionary churches, supporting dozens of works around the world. To many in the denomination, Stone was the Mother Church.

Years later, while I was serving with our denomination's youth department, I got a phone call from the highly respected Ernest C. Sumrall, a paragon of the faith and pastor of The Stone Church at the time. He needed a speaker for a series of eight services.

I did not know Sumrall nor the members of the congregation. But Greisen's words floated back through my mind: "If you're ever asked to preach . . ."

Almost with amusement, I accepted the invitation.

A year later Sumrall called me back for another eight-day series. It was during that week that his assistant pastor, Earl Henning, took me to Chicago's famous downtown district, the Loop, for my first true taste of the big city.

I had never seen Michigan Avenue. I had never seen the Merchandise Mart, nor the elevated trains, nor the Prudential Building. I was the typical saucer-eyed tourist, amazed to find myself walking faster than the traffic, up and down the famous streets. Perhaps most startling of all was Henning's suggestion that we get out of the city before 3 p.m.

"Why?" I asked.

"Because," he laughed, "when the traffic starts, everything stops!"

And that was the whole picture I had of Chicago when The Stone Church called and asked me to become their pastor.

It had been nearly six years since I had spoken there. I was not the prime candidate.

After the board had discussed the other names on their list, someone suggested that each man write the name of his first choice on a card and pass it face-down to the chairman.

All nine cards turned up bearing the same name: Owen Carr.

I hesitated to go. By this time I had been pastoring at Edwards Street over three years, and it was an immensely fulfilling work. I talked with E.M. Clark, the man in charge of the denomination's churches in Illinois, and he told me flatly that moving to Stone would be a step backwards.

"You would not want to go there," he said with unmistakable finality. "Your situation now is ideal. The church is responding to your ministry. Everything is moving beautifully.

"The Stone Church is no longer an active church—not what it once was," he added. "They are not open to new ideas. They would be very slow to make changes. You would be unhappy at The Stone Church.''

I heard his words, but I wasn't listening to his logic. I was listening instead to a quiet, persistent voice inside me. It was **the** prodding of God's Holy Spirit, that same "still, small **voice**" again. God had fastened His will to my life. He was not going to let me stay put.

Before I moved to the Chicago area, I talked with Clark again. My decision had been made, and he backed me solidly now.

"Do you think a church of 400 can make an impact on a city of seven million?" I asked him, a little apprehensively.

"I don't know," he replied softly. "But if they try and fail, I think they could be forgiven, don't you?"

It was a principle I was to share with the church board—and dozens of others—again and again in the coming months.

Chapter 7

An Apple Suspended

Dave Oseland has been a media enthusiast since before he knew the difference between radio and TV. He was somewhat of a communications prospector, poking around in all the media just to make sure he didn't miss any gold.

Channel 38 in Chicago was his biggest find.

When I met Dave, he had his fingers in several media pies. He was involved in both television and radio work, some of which took him frequently to the ninety-seventh floor of the John Hancock Building, where Dave maintained a transmitter for one of the city's television stations.

One day, long before I met him, Dave noticed workers hooking up a transmitter for a new Chicago channel. As he watched the machinery being assembled day after day, he began saying to himself, *"Wouldn't it be great to have a Christian television station in Chicago?"*

It was a far-fetched notion for Dave Oseland, who didn't know that Christian television stations existed anywhere. By some fluke, he had never even seen the "P.T.L. Club" or the "700 Club." It was clearly a pointer from the Lord, specifically for Dave Oseland, to set his faith in the direction of Christian television.

The new transmitter in the Hancock, he discovered, was for Channel 38, a virgin channel only recently granted to the Chicago Federation of Labor by the F.C.C. (They were already successful in the radio business, operating the popular WCFL-AM.)

Of course, Oseland knew that getting the channel for Christian broadcasting was the wildest of ideas. The C.F.L.

had half a million dues-paying members and the political clout to match. They had already beaten out five other interested groups to get the F.C.C. nod. No one would even consider challenging the C.F.L. for Channel 38 now, particularly since they had virtually created its machinery themselves. Besides, they held a twenty-year lease on the section of Hancock's ninety-seventh floor where their transmitter was housed, a lease that was costing them well over $60,000 a year.

But the dream hung in Dave's mind, like a luscious-looking apple suspended far, far out of reach.

As the work on the new transmitter and antenna came to a close, however, UHF television stations all over the country began sliding toward collapse. It was an unexplainable epidemic. Even in Chicago UHF stations were having financial trouble. Station managers couldn't find programing. Only a scant few of them across the country were hooked into any of the major networks. Because they couldn't find programing they couldn't find advertisers.

Suddenly the C.F.L. curbed their horses and took a long, conservative look at their project on the top of the John Hancock Building. Somehow they could no longer tune in a pretty picture. As a result, Channel 38, a brand-new, never-used, high-powered television station, went on the auction block.

I heard the news, but I also heard that Zenith Corporation almost immediately picked up an option on the station. What I did not know was that Zenith let its option expire several months later, and that again Channel 38 was up for grabs.

Dave Oseland at this point went nearly crazy with excitement. He began talking to Christian businessmen, pumping the concept of a Christian television station. Most said they were too busy. None saw the vision.

Still, the Holy Spirit was at work, making connections of the least likely sort. Oseland's manager at WYCA in Hammond was Don Hodges, who was planning to move to

Oklahoma City. Oseland relayed the information to Hodges. A few days later, as the Hodges family began circulating their final farewells among Chicago acquaintances, they spent an evening with their friends, the Joel Lundquists. Lundquist was a member of The Stone Church board and the church's Sunday School superintendent. In the course of the evening's casual conversation, Hodges mentioned the fact that Channel 38 was for sale. A few more days passed and the Lundquists found themselves at a dinner with Priscilla and me and with Richard Dortch and his wife. Dortch is head of the churches of our denomination for the state of Illinois.

"Pastor, that television station you wanted is available now," Lundquist said during a lull in the conversation.

Dortch looked up in surprise.

"I have just the contact for you!" he said. "Bob Gibson, state treasurer of the A.F.L.-C.I.O.,*—the C.F.L.'s parent organization—is a boyhood friend of mine. We grew up on the same block together in Granite City."

So from Oseland to Hodges to Lundquist to Dortch to Gibson to the Chicago Federation of Labor it went—and all via the Holy Spirit. Truly God appeared to be leading.

Bob Gibson would prove to be a very powerful politician and a vital link to the C.F.L. in the long negotiations ahead. And Dave Oseland was far from being finished with the dream. His part had only begun.

The first meeting with the C.F.L. officials was no harbinger of spring. William Lee, president of the C.F.L., a grandfatherly gentleman in his seventies, saw the schoolboy foolishness of our plans.

"Reverend, you couldn't afford to own it," he said to me with a condescending smile. "And even if you could afford to own it, you couldn't afford to operate it."

It was a closed case in Lee's mind.

At the end of the meeting I read him a poem which I always carry in my wallet.

---

*American Federation of Labor and Congress of Industrial Organizations.

If you want a thing bad enough
To go out and fight for it—
Work day and night for it—
Give up your time, and your peace and sleep
for it—
If only desire of it makes you quite mad enough
never to tire of it;
Makes you hold all other things tawdry and cheap
for it,
If gladly you'll sweat for it, fret for it, plan for it,
Lose all your terror of the devil and man for it;
If you'll simply go after that thing that you want
With all your capacity, strength and sagacity,
Faith, hope, and confidence, stern pertinacity;
If neither cold, poverty, famished and gaunt,
Nor sickness, nor pain of body or brain
Can turn you away from the thing that you want,
If, dogged and grim, you besiege and beset it—
MY BROTHER, YOU'LL GET IT!!

Then I prayed with him and left.

It could have been disheartening, except that Taylor Davis, our assistant pastor at The Stone Church, was with me. On the way out of the building he grinned. "Boy, it's going to happen. It's really going to happen!" he said.

Somehow I knew in that moment that Taylor was as good as any prophet.

In the following weeks, a surprised C.F.L. found us knocking on their door again and again. No proposal they could make would keep us from coming back. No proposal we could make would give them pause. We had no money, no corporation, no assets, no promoters, no backers, and no prospects for any of the above.

It became very clear, and quickly, that we were going to need that spark of excitement from a body of believers.

We were about to find out whether a few hundred people could be forgiven for trying to make an impact on several million. Or whether they would even be willing to risk it.

Chapter 8

Letting Out the Cat

Springing the idea of owning a television station on The Stone Church was just the thing to upset my ministerial apple cart.

In the three years since my first Sunday at Stone, the church had nearly doubled in size; the people were growing in enthusiasm; God was blessing the local ministry.

But the staff, the board and I began planning to spring loose the monster anyway, regardless of the popularity risk. If this were to be a disaster, we were determined to make it of titanic proportions.

We needed a unique presentation, a package unlike any other ever seen at The Stone Church, to tell the whole story from its inception.

To produce such a package, we called in a unique individual, also unlike any other ever seen at The Stone Church: a highly creative Christian artist named Lloyd Colbaugh.

Like an innovative Jonah, Colbaugh spent three days and three nights behind locked doors, writing and drawing and painting. When he emerged, he had created a gripping masterpiece of audio-visual drama—"The City With No Doors."

We began promoting Sunday morning, September 30, 1973, as the single most exciting event anyone would ever experience at The Stone Church. Between the board members and the staff members and myself, we saturated the congregation with the news: something sensational, something colossal was on its way, scheduled to arrive Sunday, September 30, at 9:30 a.m.

No one was to miss this service. We trucked in twenty-eight teenagers from the neighboring Calvary Temple in Flossmoor, to take care of all the children during the service. We invited editor Bill Bray of *Chicago Church News* to attend. We blacked out the windows, and at nine-thirty that morning we locked the doors.

The choir, primed to the point of nervous frenzy for the mysterious special occasion, opened the service by singing "The King Is Coming." About 700 were present that morning when I opened my Bible to Jesus' final instructions to His followers. I wanted this project to be introduced on good authority.

"Go ye into all the world," I began reading in Mark 16, "and preach the Gospel to every creature."

And I told a little story:

"They say when Jesus returned to heaven, after living and dying and rising again on earth, that the angels gathered around Him and asked Him what it was like to live on earth. So He told them about His life, and His work, and His purpose—to take the message of salvation to all the world.

"'But how do you plan to do that,' they asked Him, 'now that you've left the earth?'

"'I chose twelve men,' Jesus replied, 'and I left my message with them to take to the rest of the world.'

"The angels were silent for a moment. Then one of them asked quietly, 'What if they fail?'

"And Jesus replied, 'I have no other plan.'

"The Great Commission is up to us to fulfill," I told the people. "Ordinary folks are the ones Jesus gave the job to."

The time had come. With the tension of anticipation pulling at every breath, I introduced the event.

"Today we stand ready to unveil to you what God has laid upon our hearts...

"Imagine...a city with no doors. Where race or color would be no barrier. Nor wealth. Nor lack of it. Where we would reach people in their serious, most intimate moment, hidden away from the throng, from the pressures of the busy day..."

The sanctuary was silent, with every pair of eyes fastened on the great pages of pictures prepared by Lloyd. I flipped them one by one.

"To television," I read, "Chicago is already that city. Its unseen waves vibrate in every hidden corner, behind every forbidding door.

"In the most dismal skid-row bar.

"In comfortable, self-satisfied, middle-class Chicagoland.

"In the poshest apartment.

"All barriers are melted away—and the city lies exposed in all its crying need..."

A stream of possibilities followed: Christian marriage counseling for Chicago families via television. Help for Chicago's drug addicts, Chicago's alcoholics, via television. Worship for the city's shut-ins, the city's invalids, the city's hospitalized, via television.

I talked about the state of television. "Moral rot has crept into program after program. Why not have clean entertainment as an alternative?" I asked.

Christian programs for young people. Christian programs for the aged. Christian programs for the deaf. Christian programs for the everyday, average Christian!

"Building churches is like digging wells," I continued, "when what we need to do is release a floodtide!

"Chicago is the City With No Doors! The City With No Doors is ours for the taking! We can have it—if we take it.

"But we must act now.

"If we do not act within days, other voices and other scenes will be on that station...will claim the loyalties and the allegiance of this City With No Doors!"

The lights came on. The congregation sat still and silent. I told them about Channel 38, the dark channel available for Christian television.

"If we visualize The Stone Church as a tent," I said simply, returning to the old allusion, "our tent reaches out over a thousand people. But if we can lengthen our cords, if we can strengthen our stakes, we can build a bigger tent and cover more people.

"Television is like a tent too," I explained. "From the top of the John Hancock Building in downtown Chicago, the television tent stretches eighty miles in every direction and covers more than eight million souls.

"What The Stone Church is doing today is like what David did to Goliath. God could have stricken Goliath with a heart attack," I said with a shrug, "and he could have dropped dead. But God didn't do that. He sent a little fellow out there to take care of that giant."

Still silence in the sanctuary.

"What we're doing today is like what Gideon did with his 300 men. God could have sent lightning bolts into the Midianite camp and destroyed 135,000 warriors. But instead God chose a scared country boy and gave him 300 untrained assistants. They were outnumbered 450-to-one, but they scored a magnificent victory."

But I wanted to bring it all home. I wanted each person listening to my words to realize what his own stake was in this dream.

"Today, we make an investment in our own," I told them. "Our own lives. Our own well-being. Our own children, our own grandchildren. Our neighbors, our friends, our city. We make an investment in our own...

"And," I added, "we estimate it will take an investment of $4,000,000. Up front."

I was astonished at the response of the audience. Many were weeping.

The deacons distributed preprinted envelopes, then began collecting them as they were filled with gifts.

Each offering was taken first by a board member, then handed to a staff member, and finally passed along to me—to make sure every gift was counted properly.

I had arranged for a trumpet trio to blast a fanfare as we passed each $10,000. But before anyone could stop to think about fanfares, the congregation had given $70,000.

We soon passed the $80,000 mark, and then $90,000, and then $100,000.

But the people continued to give even more, cheerfully,

tearfully, as their awed pastor watched and wept and praised God. Two and a half hours after we had begun, the people of The Stone Church had given $135,000 in cash and ninety-day pledges.

Editor Bill Bray stood up with a flushed face and exclaimed, "I have *never* seen anything so *exciting* in all my *life*!"

The entire sanctuary was supercharged with the electricity of victory. We shouted and praised God. It was a major milestone in the life of every person present. Nothing would ever duplicate the incredible move of God through His people on that Sunday morning.

Chapter 9

Opposition Like a Flood

The next day a widow stepped into my office and laid $2,000 in cash on my desk. It clearly represented much of her total worth. I didn't want to accept it, but I realized that the burdens would have to be shared if the blessings were also to fall freely.

When I told Priscilla about the incident, she looked worried.

"How will you ever face these people," she asked me gravely, "if you don't get this station on the air, and then you can't pay them back?"

"I can't afford to think about it," I replied.

One deacon's wife was so excited she couldn't sleep for three nights.

For a while I was riding high on the crest of victory too. Within a week we incorporated Christian Communications of Chicagoland under the law of the State of Illinois, with The Stone Church deacons serving as the corporation's board of directors. We opened an account with an impressive initial deposit. We started printing a newsletter. We hired local legal counsel and an F.C.C. attorney in Washington.

One of the first actions of the C.C.C. board was to hire a vice president for marketing and development. His official assignment was to promote the project and raise funds. His assignment in my words was to "put us on the air." By either standard it was a mammoth task.

For the position we selected Steve Warner, one of the finest young men ever to attend The Stone Church. He came to us with a freshly completed master's degree in com-

Priscilla and Owen Carr in their wedding picture in 1942.

Loaded to the windows, the Chevy Coupe waits to take the Carrs to Gerlane, Kansas, for their first pastorate.

Owen and Priscilla stand on the porch of the parsonage in Gerlane.

The fateful meeting between representatives of the boards of directors of the Chicago Federation of Labor and Christian Communications of Chicagoland, Inc. which finalized arrangements for the operation of Christian Channel 38 in Chicago.

Some of the men who worked to make possible Christian TV in Chicago gather in the studio to savor the triumph of the first evening on the air. Left to right: Jerry Rose, Richard Weidmann, Robert Hart, Max Ephraim, Owen Carr, Fred Severance, Kenneth Swanson. (Peter J. Haas)

The John Hancock Building, which houses Channel 38's transmitter, rises above its neighbors on the Chicago skyline. (Chicago Assn. of Commerce & Industry/Kee T. Chang)

A page from the Bible, Genesis 1, was the first official picture broadcast on Channel 38.

Left to right, Paul Crouch, president of Trinity Broadcasting Network in California (Channel 40), Owen Carr, Jerry Rose, and Pastor Morrow of The Stone Church share a laugh during the first airing of "Chicago," Channel 38's nightly talk show.

Jerry Rose (left), general manager of Channel 38, and Owen Carr, president, on the set of "Chicago."

Jerry Rose and Owen Carr chat with Richard Flessing and Jim Bakker (right center), of "PTL Club." In the background counselors take phone calls from viewers.

munications from Wheaton College. Steve was ideal for the job.

But starting big was not God's ideal for us.

Opposition rolled over us like tidal waves almost from the day we went public. Church leaders sneered. Laymen laughed us off. Men with business experience gave us twenty reasons why the dream was doomed.

The Sunday following the "City With No Doors" presentation, WYCA in Hammond broadcast taped excerpts from the service. Before long a radio preacher in suburban South Holland was telling Chicago in blunt terms that we were wasting God's money by trying to establish a Christian television station.

Bill Bray gave us good coverage in *Chicago Church News*. But Chicagoland's newspaper columnists gave us a different reception, everything from ho hum to ho-ho-ho.

Ron Powers, columnist for the big *Chicago Sun-Times*, devoted a day's worth of writing to the subject, concluding that the odds for our success were "at this point somewhat long."

"The Reverend Owen Carr," the sarcastic column began, "is a man who believes there ought to be some decent television in Chicago, for Christ's sake." It went on for the full length of the page in the same vein.

Neutral stories were invariably much shorter. Supportive press coverage was sporadic. *Christian Life* magazine gave us two noncommittal paragraphs.

We were in trouble.

I felt like the biblical David as I packed up the "City With No Doors" flip chart and turned into the wind. David, too, was the least among his brothers. Even his father considered him insignificant. When the prophet Samuel came to the house for a meal, David's father didn't even call him from the fields.

When Samuel began looking among Jesse's sons for someone to become the next king, he would have chosen any one of the older ones. He was unimpressed with the youngest. But on God's instruction, Samuel anointed David as king.

It was this unlikely call of God that I carried with me as I began knocking on doors, talking to pastors and civic leaders and businessmen and laymen and—eventually—anyone who would give me two minutes back-to-back to spell out the concept. Many people were interested but not many to the point of giving. Many were apathetic. Many couldn't trust something they couldn't see or touch.

David, I realized, had the same trouble with his brothers. They were soldiers in the king's army, and when David brought them food, they sneered at him. He was out of place among the mighty men of Israel. But God saw within each man: they looked like great warriors, but they had the hearts of cowards. Only the "stripling" had the heart of a king.

Over and over I spelled out the facts—to ladies' groups, at business luncheons, at club socials—a shepherd before soldiers. Again and again I told of the dream of a Christian television station in Chicago. And over and over the first question was, "Now, will this be an hour or a half-hour?"

Sometimes it seemed that nobody would ever understand.

But David's words rang true in my heart: "The battle is the Lord's" (I Samuel 17:47). It was this confidence in God's power that led David victoriously through the battle with Goliath. And it was this same confidence I determined to demonstrate. God had clearly directed me to bring Christian television to Chicago, and now soldiers or no, I was going to see the battle through.

Like David, I felt myself drawing closer and closer to the heart of God. Almost daily I could feel more and more of the intimacy of the Psalms, David's love-songs to the Father. I recognized it as an intimacy of years, of tears, spawned in crisis.

The board members of our infant corporation began scrambling for leads on potential contributors. Every lead was followed up. No stone, no matter how far-fetched, was left unturned.

One day a man called to congratulate me on my courage. His company, he said, wanted to make a "sizable contribution." Could I come to his office in the suburbs to discuss this contribution? I certainly could.

It was a lovely telephone conversation, but as I hung up I felt a wave of nausea. Something was rotten in this suburbia.

Before long I placed a worried call to Lex Young, the C.F.L. engineer, who was a long-time Chicagoan.

I gave Lex the name of the man's company. Lex didn't recognize it. Odd, I thought.

Then I gave Lex the name of the man, and he began shouting into the phone: "Stay away from that man! He's dangerous!"

I was stunned. "What do you mean by 'dangerous'?" I asked.

"I mean he's under investigation by the authorities!" Lex replied, almost angrily. "He's been known to break people's legs with a baseball bat!"

What could I do with the meeting I had set up? At the moment of crisis I revealed a deep strength that is common to many corporate leaders: I asked my secretary, Elaine Wilson, to cancel for me.

Only one fund-raising incident was ever to rival that one for spine-tingling. It happened months later, when, with the fund-raising effort still floundering, a concerned woman in The Stone Church arranged for us to meet with a "rich Mexican" businessman in downtown Chicago. The businessman's "banker" turned out to be a wheeler-dealer from Las Vegas.

Minutes into the meeting I realized I was at the center of an underworld summit conference. The Mexican businessman wanted to house our ministry in his building as a laundering operation for his money.

Time slowed down to an agonizing crawl. Each minute yawned and stretched and lazed its way around the clock. When I knew it must be after nine, I glanced at my wristwatch. It was only seven.

The businessman turned to the banker in a real-life scene from a gangster movie and asked him, "Are you with me in this?"

The banker knew his cue. "I'm with you," he replied.

The businessman turned back to me. "You can have a million dollars on Monday."

Seven years later I would still not have raised my first million dollars for Christian television. And I could have had a cool million in underworld money in three days.

I put my papers in my briefcase, thanked the gentlemen for their kindness in listening, stood up with the lady, and walked out.

In a final touch of Hollywood, the businessman sent a burly bodyguard with us to the car. He stood and watched us until our car was on its way. Needless to say, I did not let the well-meaning lady make any more appointments for me.

Negotiations with the C.F.L. dragged on and on. The three-month target date came and went as we entered 1974. I had not raised $4,000,000. And the Chicago Federation of Labor had not agreed to sell for what we had added to our bank account: a little over $20,000.

Promoters were hired and fired with alarming regularity. One lasted six weeks and proved ineffective. Another came to us with excellent contacts in the money world. He spent a few months on payroll, zigzagging across Chicagoland, making hundreds of contacts, producing nothing. One man had an excellent track record for fund-raising in other parts of the country. In Chicago he was helpless.

I was learning the hard way to seek God's face even in the most trivial matters.

Support from Chicagoland's churches was tentative, sporadic, threadbare. As the summer of '74 heated up, we had taken in only one 25th of the $4,000,000 dollars we needed.

"The City With No Doors" was nine months behind us now. The momentum of that morning had evaporated.

But there were also positive strokes in the long, long year of 1974—although they seemed to spread themselves fairly thin. Early in the year, the board reorganized itself to include members from a cross-section of the city. Some of The Stone Church men graciously resigned to make room for new people to serve with us.

One of the sharpest controversies over Christian television in Chicago was whether it would be controlled by The Stone Church, and if so what would be the program content? We concluded that our programs should present Jesus Christ as the Son of God and the Savior of mankind. Without being born-again through faith in Him, a person would be lost. We also agreed that we should not limit our theological content to any special doctrine but appeal to the entire evangelical community.

One great stride forward marked the summer of 1974. The First National Bank of Evergreen Park gave us a letter of credit for $600,000, boosting our assets and our spirits simultaneously. Our position with the C.F.L. improved somewhat—but not enough. We were still in different leagues.

Chapter 10

"Let's Admit We Tried and Failed"

Prospects for 1975 were less inviting than even those of the previous tempestuous year. The excitement of "The City With No Doors" was a dim, somewhat sad memory.

I was late for the first board meeting of the New Year. By the time I arrived, the meeting had taken a gloomy turn. *We've tried everything,* the conversation went, *every angle, every idea we could think of. And we're no closer today than we were when we began two and a half years ago.*

When I arrived, the men were tossing back and forth a list of conditions that they thought would keep the project reasonably alive. If the conditions didn't improve within ninety days, they were prepared to dump the project.

A few hundred people couldn't make an impact on several million after all. Let's admit that we tried and failed.

As the mountain of despair grew I decided to go with the flow. I asked for more comments, and urged the men to express all the doubts they had been harboring. I expressed no opinions. At the close of the meeting the assumption was that we were through, done, washed up. The next board meeting (perhaps the final one) would be in two weeks.

I had not talked to anyone about the previous meeting when I opened this one. I felt weighted down as I spoke.

"We have been in this a long time," I began slowly, looking around the room. "Over four years for me. Three years for Max. Two years for Cecil and Fred. Over a year for Steve . . ." I paused.

"Many others would have quit before now. As we know, other groups did start and quit...

"It appears that we too are beginning to wind this thing down. The statement was made in the last meeting that if certain things do not happen by a certain date, we have no choice but to write off the project. To abort it...

"Permit me to verbalize my inner feelings on the matter. Under no circumstances should we even consider the possibility of aborting the project. We may have to come at it from a hundred directions before we finally whip it. But let's not stop—short of death, the rapture, or success.

"Knowing how I got into this, I have no intention of winding it down, closing it out, or aborting it. This is not a burden for which I volunteered. I feel drafted of the Lord."

I paused. The members sat in a mild state of shock.

I proceeded to tell them about a meeting I had attended in the past week with Steve Warner. The meeting included three high-profile Christian leaders of the Chicago area. They had made some strong, aggressive recommendations for moving the project ahead, which I immediately suggested to the nine surprised board members.

I recommended that we should select a fifty-member Board of Reference, big names in the religious circles of Chicago who could simply grace our letterhead. Also we should enlarge our official working board to twenty members who would more fully represent a cross-section of Chicagoland. And we should select from this board an executive committee of seven men to run the corporation.

No one spoke. No one shook off the surprise.

My recommendations were carried unanimously. The meeting ended, and the men began to leave by twos and threes.

Only one man stopped—Cecil Swanson, the board's secretary.

"We needed to hear that," he said to me quietly. "We needed to see how strongly you felt about this."

Perhaps, I said to myself, the new three-board plan will provide the spark we so desperately needed...But no, we

69

discovered in the next few weeks, the new plan would not provide a spark of any kind. The Christian television project could not even find fifty willing names to fill up its letterhead.

Nobody wanted to be a part of anything so stupid.

Many times the C.F.L. hesitated to talk about the station without the presence of their attorney, James Greeley, who was conveniently located within walking distance of the F.C.C.—in Washington, D.C. It cost the C.F.L. $1,000 a day plus expenses to fly him in to Chicago.

In August of 1975, after months of haggling and stalling, I decided to intercept the psychological football and go on the offensive. I proposed to President Lee that we fly to Washington and do business in Greeley's own office. Okay, he said, and we set the date.

The next Sunday night I stood in the pulpit of The Stone Church. I looked out at a congregation who knew nothing of the crisis we were facing. I could not share it with them; the time was not yet right.

But they could pray regardless of what they knew. I had seen the power of united prayer at work my entire life, and now it was time to focus that power on the Chicago Federation of Labor.

In that service, I passed out 100 white index cards with a single sentence printed on each one: "Tomorrow at 2 p.m., I'll be in prayer for you." The hundred people who took the cards made the promise without knowing where I would be at 2 p.m. the next day.

The next morning I drew a check for $25,000 at the church. It was 6 a.m. when I knocked on Deacon Ken Swanson's door for his signature. Then I headed for O'Hare Airport and to Washington.

I sat in that plane and felt sorry for the men I would be facing in the capital. The Holy Spirit, the Paraclete, the one called alongside, was sitting with me, dealing for me in these men's hearts. They had no earthly equivalent to the swaying power of God's Holy Spirit. They couldn't cope. They didn't have a chance. My own spirit was calm.

When I sat down in James Greeley's office, we were $1,000,000 apart. The C.F.L. price had dropped slowly over the weeks from the original figure of $2,000,000, but I was still down in the six-figure area. And only barely.

It was a wide gap to bridge, but a Master Bridge-builder was at work in that room.

As the figures were laid out, Lee's eyebrows drew together sharply.

"Reverend!" he said, genuinely shocked at the gulf between the two numbers. "I can't give you a $1,000,000 of union dues!"

I talked some more. I cajoled and nudged. I talked soft and then tough and tried every tactic I could think of to keep the conversation alive. But eventually the talk wore thin.

Lee finally said, "I thought you wanted to do business! Why did we even fly in here?"

"To let you know I *mean* business," I replied evenly. It was time for the ace-up-the-sleeve. I pulled the $25,000 check out of my pocket and tossed it on Greeley's desk.

Surprise! They didn't expect me to have money in hand.

"Of course, I realize that $25,000 doesn't mean a great deal to you gentlemen," I said, pressing the advantage, "but I'm prepared to turn this money over to you as irrevocable collateral, with an agreement to produce the balance of whatever figure we agree on."

Lee stammered a moment. I knew he could go two ways: he could either accept the check, or he could laugh it off as chicken feed.

"Oh, Reverend, I'm sorry," he said after a moment, "but you'd have to come up with at least another ...."

I expected to hear something in the millions.

".... At least another $150,000."

I sighed, happily. I excused myself to place a conference call to the board members. Fred Severance, Max Ephraim, and Cecil Swanson were all on the line as I laid out the proposed down payment. "I don't even have to pray about that agreement!" Fred said excitedly. "Sign it!"

After two years, we finally had a break in the clouds.

Desperate to keep moving, the board had packed Steve Warner off on a fact-finding trip that summer, writing up an itinerary of media ministries in eight states across the South and West. His instructions were simple: "Learn how to do it."

Steve returned with two hot items that were destined to change our television picture entirely.

One was a revised budget. He had pared down our $4,000,000 starting figure by changing our plans—based on what other ministries had done while they were still trying to get off the ground. It was the bittersweet way to reach our goal—pulling the target toward the archer—but it would speed up our plans nonetheless.

The other hot item Steve brought back was simply a name. It was a name destined to be linked as closely as my own to the Christian television project in Chicagoland, a name that would propel the dream of Channel 38 into reality.

The name was Jerry Rose.

Yes, I was looking desperately for help. But I also was aware that help must come in the form of a man called by God. It is impossible to overestimate the value God places upon a man of His choosing.

When God started to populate the earth, He started with one man.

Many nations already existed when God was ready to choose a nation through which the blessing of a Redeemer would come. But God selected one man, Abraham. He gave him one son, Isaac. He gave Isaac two sons, and rejected one of them—dealing for three generations with only one man.

When God needed to spare His small company, seventy souls, he sent Joseph into Egypt to be on hand when he was needed.

When that company multiplied to millions, and needed deliverance from bondage, God prepared Moses, and sent him on the impossible mission.

The highest estimate placed on the value of man is that when God needed a Redeemer to save man from his sins, God's own Son became a man. Not an angel. Not royalty. Just a common man.

Before the Redeemer came, God wanted to prepare the hearts of the people for this exciting intrusion of divinity into the affairs of human history. So He sent a man. "There was a man sent from God, whose name was John" (John 1:6).

God always has His man. He prepares him. Often in obscurity. Then brings him to the scene of conflict at His own appointed time.

Unknown to me, God had a Jerry Rose. He had chosen him. Prepared him.

The background and training of Moses and Aaron were as different as could be. They had one thing in common—the same parents. Everything else was different. Yet, as Moses was enroute to Pharaoh's palace, God sent Aaron to meet him. Now with two-thirds of their lives behind them, God brought them together. Instantly their lives meshed in God's work and will. They would spend the balance of their lives fulfilling God's will in ministering to His people.

Jerry and I had only one thing in common—the same Heavenly Father. Our ancestry, our education, our training were all different. But immediately there was compatibility. Total strangers suddenly flowing with one heart and one spirit. A common purpose. Guided by the same principles.

With Moses, the lot was cast. He had heard from God at the burning bush. He was enroute to Pharaoh when Aaron met him in the wilderness.

With me, the application had been filed. We were anticipating owning a TV station and I knew absolutely nothing about television. As I walked uncertainly toward the biggest tests of my life, God sent Jerry Rose to meet me in my wilderness.

"There was a man sent from God" applies to more than just John the Baptist. It applied to Jerry Rose, and it can apply to you.

Chapter 11

Babylon

Jerry Rose told me no. He was "not free to make a move." In other words, he wasn't interested.

But I was becoming a desperate man. As every day passed, I discovered more and more of how little I knew about what I was doing. I could barely carry on a conversation with anyone in the television industry—because I didn't understand the jargon!

After stalling out in virtually every aspect of the television project—and now even Steve Warner had resigned to pastor a new local church—I had only one promise to hang onto. "God hath chosen the foolish things of the world to confound the wise," Paul writes in I Corinthians 1, "and God hath chosen the weak things of the world to confound the things which are mighty; and base things of the world, and things which are despised, hath God chosen, yea, and things which are not, to bring to nought things that are: That no flesh should glory in his presence."

By 1975 I had no reason to glory in anything.

But one of the kindest things God can do for a servant who doesn't know anything is to send him a helper who does. Moses was incompetent when it came to public speaking. God kindly sent Aaron to meet him in the wilderness. Owen Carr was incompetent when it came to television. God kindly sent Jerry Rose—eventually—to meet me in my wilderness.

Jerry could not have special-ordered a more perfect background in television work. A serious-minded Texan, Jerry felt God calling him early into a lifetime of television work. He conscientiously began his career at the bottom—as a floor-sweeper and general flunkie at an educational television station in Dallas. It was the lowest beginning possible in the media world of 1963.

But by the time he left educational television, Jerry Rose had begun the long climb upward. He was the station's chief announcer when he resigned to do a stint in radio.

Before long, Jerry was back in television, this time at the ABC Network affiliate in Dallas. He began as a cameraman, moved to scenic designing, and finally became the station's lighting director.

Here he did Wide World of Sports coverage, National Football League remotes, and a wide variety of other work. Then Jerry moved to Channel 39 in Dallas, an independent UHF station owned by Doubleday Broadcasting. When he left the station he had been promoted five times—finally to the position of producer-director.

Jerry left Dallas to become program and operations manager for a CBS affiliate in El Paso.

From there he went to Channel 33 in Dallas—a station which Christian Broadcasting Network had just bought. Jerry's assignment was to put the station on the air. It was an assignment that would prove to be invaluable background for his later work. Later C.B.N. moved its Dallas operation to Channel 39, where Jerry became general manager.

After a decade of television work, having held almost every post there is to hold in a television station, Jerry Rose was not missing much in terms of experience. No resume could be more complete. He was precisely what we needed to solve all of our problems—I thought.

When Steve Warner returned from his fact-finding tour in the summer of '74, he returned with a sweeping analysis: "In all my contacts, I have only met one real professional in Christian television. His name is Jerry Rose."

The chemistry was already cooking between our family and Jerry. When Steve had arrived in Dallas, looking for someone to talk with about Christian television, he and Jerry became instant brothers.

A beautiful rapport drew them together in the Spirit.

Jerry Rose is a generally private person. He has never made it a habit to invite strangers into his home. But that evening Jerry brought his new friend home to meet his family and talk more with him—into the small hours of the morning—about Christian television.

The project was draining me. I felt the pressure to get back into the mainstream of activities at The Stone Church. Over and over I found myself saying, "I'll be glad when we get this station on the air, so I can go back to pastoring."

I desperately needed someone who could close the C.F.L. deal, put the station on the air, and then keep it there.

"Lord, give me someone," I prayed.

I saw Jerry Rose as that perfect someone who could solve all my problems. I called him. Jerry and his family were no longer in Dallas. Pat Robertson, founder of CBN, had pulled him into the Portsmouth, Virginia, headquarters to manage the operations of the entire Christian Broadcasting Network.

Had I known of Jerry's other offers, I might never have called him. Prominent evangelists and singers had asked him to join their staffs. Television stations—Christian and commercial—had made him offers.

Jerry also had ideas of his own. He wanted to spin his wide knowledge of television into a ministry of its own—a company that would help pastors use television to the best advantage.

And I had no good reason for Jerry to consider leaving Virginia in favor of Chicago. I had little to offer him—no money to speak of, no organization to speak of. I wanted him to take over a television station that didn't even exist yet.

But "not many wise, not many mighty..." I called early one morning, before Jerry had left for work. He was polite. He said he would give it some thought.

Actually, he had recoiled at the idea of moving to Chicago. Jerry and his family were living in Virginia Beach, across the street from the Atlantic Ocean, and they loved it.

There was no locale in the entire country where they would rather live than the Tidewater area of Virginia. They had long, beautiful summers and short, mild winters. They had miles and miles of beaches. Jerry had the boats and the sea that he loved. He had sailing and surfing and marlin fishing, and what else could a man ask for?

When Jerry hung up and told his wife Shirley about the call, her eyes opened wide and fearful.

"Not Chicago," she said, with an urgent, silent "please" dropped in behind.

Neither of the two knew anything about Chicago. Neither wanted to find out.

But the Holy Spirit was at work. Jerry was in Dallas the next week—doing the first trial runs on his television seminars for pastors—when he called me back and told me he would fly up to discuss the project. I believe he was too intrigued with the entire concept of Christian television not to inspect a situation like ours.

The board assembled to meet him. After months of promoting this foreign concept to deaf and puzzled ears, Jerry's conversation sounded refreshingly like a recording of my own words.

Then Max and Audrey Ephraim took Jerry downtown to see the transmitter in the Hancock. In classic style, it turned out that Christian Communications of Chicagoland, Inc., did not have a key to get in to the transmitter. As a weak second choice, the Ephraims took Jerry to the Hancock's observation deck.

Inside, Jerry's heart was gripped by the sight of the city. He squinted into the distance and could not see anything but houses, apartments, offices, shops—people. Suddenly, he told us later, he had the vague feeling that he might come to this city and *fail*.

Outwardly, though, Jerry was obviously not overwhelmed by a burden for Chicago. The yachts lying at anchor in the marina were neat, he said. He did not talk too much about the millions of souls and the prospects of reaching them.

But he was ill at ease. Chicago was Babylon. It was the

great filthy city. Besides, Jerry and Shirley were native Southerners. Why should they move to the North?

As we parted, Jerry declined the offer.

I was deflated, but I clutched at a last-chance possibility—anything to salvage some positive results from the encounter. Could he recommend someone to us, I asked, who could do the job as well as he could?

Jerry said he would contact me with his recommendations. Good-bye.

Lord, give me someone.

The old, desperate prayer grew hollow. Not long after Jerry left, I knew I would have to fill the old hollow prayer with fresh oil.

Lord, give me Jerry Rose. Make Jerry Rose feel for this city what You have made me feel for it.

Jerry went home. "Well," Shirley asked him, "what did you think?"

"Not much."

Two days later Shirley was lying on the bed, staring across the room.

"Jerry, we are going to Chicago."

"No, I don't believe we are."

It was embarrassing for Jerry to come up with a list of people he would recommend for the job. He couldn't think of anyone else qualified to do the job. Talented television insiders form a small club.

So he stalled. For weeks he did not call me back.

Meanwhile Jerry and Shirley committed themselves more heavily to the Tidewater area. They bought a house in Portsmouth, right down the street from where the *Merrimac* was sunk. They were only minutes from Williamsburg and Jamestown. Kitty Hawk and Cape Hatteras were just down the coast. The historical value of the area made Jerry love it even more.

They moved in, got involved in a local church. The people were friendly. Jerry got out his tool box and added a thousand square feet to the attic.

The Roses should have been supremely content.

But no. There was a problem somewhere. A restlessness in the house. An edge.

For the first time in their marriage, Jerry and Shirley did not enjoy their home. There was a foreign character to life there—something neither of them could describe. When they visited friends, they lingered too long. They didn't want to go back to their own house.

They loved Virginia, but they could not settle in.

Perhaps God did not want them getting too comfortable there.

The Chicago project kept knocking on Jerry's mental door. It was the worst offer he had—the biggest headache imaginable, as television jobs go. Chicago didn't jibe with Jerry's plans to be a success in Christian television.

But that also made Chicago the greatest leap of faith.

Lord, give me Jerry Rose. Make him love Chicago as You have made me love it.

It was nearly three months after our meeting when Jerry finally called, exasperated, to give me his recommendations.

"Look, I have not been able to come up with anybody I could recommend to you," he told me. "I'm sorry. I tried. I just can't come up with anybody that I could recommend."

I saw Jerry in the unusual position of being the best in his business and it was an uncomfortable position for him at the moment.

"Has the job been filled?" he asked me, hoping against hope that it had.

"No, it hasn't."

"Well, I was just checking."

An hour later the Holy Spirit tapped me on the shoulder. "Hey, I've answered your prayers."

Suddenly I realized what was happening in Jerry's heart. I grabbed the phone and dialed his number.

"Did you ask about the job being open because you're interested in filling it?"

Jerry hem-hawed. "I don't know," he hedged. "I'm praying about it."

"Jerry, we were waiting for you," I said.

Lord, give me Jerry Rose. Grip his heart for Chicagoland as You have gripped mine.

The hook had lodged. Jerry called me back and told me he wanted to visit again—this time with his wife. She had never been to Chicago before.

It was October, perhaps the loveliest month of the year in the state of Virginia. The leaves were turning their deepest, most beautiful oranges and golds.

Chicago is ugly in October. The naked trees give it a dingy look. Gray. Stark. Drab.

"Jerry, the Lord wouldn't do this to us, would He?" Shirley asked.

"I don't know," Jerry said with a shrug. "Maybe He would."

Then Shirley too saw the sprawling need of the city. She saw for the first time the miles and miles of concrete and brick, the vast urban jungle of highrises and houses. Thousands and millions of people. She was shocked, also impressed.

The Holy Spirit was moving beautifully during that weekend. Jerry finally perceived the burden I had been bearing for Chicagoland. Shirley grasped it immediately. All the way back to Virginia, they talked about Chicago. They had never seen a dream so deeply etched.

I offered Jerry the presidency of the station. I certainly didn't want it myself. I knew Jerry was capable of it. I saw him as a man I could support in running the television ministry long after I had returned to the safe harbor of The Stone Church.

Oddly, however, Jerry had the same impression of me.

"I saw in Owen Carr a man that I could follow," he would write later. That made little sense to me. I considered Jerry to be a television professional of high caliber. But God was kneading Jerry's will in His hands, taking complete control of Jerry's life and aligning the ministry to fit His will.

Jerry spent a long, long time deciding. He wanted to be very careful not to toy with the call of God on his life. Furthermore, he did not want a blot on his resume, and at the moment that was what Chicago looked to become. Did Jerry Rose really want to sacrifice sure success for the risky project?

One day he stood in the C.B.N. studios praying with the rest of the crew. He had promised me an answer by 4 p.m. that day.

"God, God, I must have an answer right now," Jerry prayed, anguished.

As he prayed, he thumbed through his Bible and came across the book of Isaiah, the same book that God had used to strike the opening chord in my own heart.

"Arise, shine," Jerry read at the opening of chapter 60, "for thy light is come, and the glory of the Lord is risen upon thee."

The Holy Spirit began speaking to Jerry's heart. He knew the words were specifically for him.

"The sun shall no more be thy light by day," he read, "neither for brightness shall the moon give light unto thee. But the Lord shall be unto thee an everlasting light, and thy God thy glory."

Jerry stopped. He looked at the past months. He had been trying to sort out his life and his ministry on his own professional terms. He was looking for a ministry, yes—but a ministry guaranteed to be successful. Any of his other offers were well within his talented grasp. Only Chicago gave him a deep-seated fear of failure.

"Jerry, you are going to do My task, not yours. It's going to be so far beyond what you are able to accomplish that you're just going to have to relax and trust Me and let Me do it My way."

Jerry knew that God had spoken through His Word. So he began to pray, "If this is Your will, Lord, then quicken it even further to my heart."

Gradually Jerry also began to be comfortable just knowing that Jesus loved him. Success—even in the ministry—was no prerequisite with the Heavenly Father.

Jerry realized that the stamp of Chicago on his heart was unmistakeable. The Lord's leading did not change.

"Hello, Owen? We will come to Chicago."

Hallelujah! God gave us Jerry Rose!

Great relief swept over me. I felt Jerry could do anything that needed to be done. Soon, I thought, I could lay the burden down. Jerry was my Superman—for the moment.

Jerry insisted on only one condition: he would not agree to become president of the station. He felt I could hold that title. He would agree to join us as vice-president and general manager.* I praised God anyway. I had no idea how crucial that decision of Jerry's would turn out to be.

Jerry knew how little we had. He began to make deals with God. He would wait for the money to come in, he thought at first, so we could have a station and a license to operate it in hand when he arrived. But God spoke to him about it: *"I have told you I will do it. Where is your faith?"*

So Jerry decided to launch out in faith, leaving behind his job security, and move to Chicago without the station, without the funds to guarantee getting it. He would leave Shirley and the children behind, and after the station was on the air they would sell the house and move.

But God spoke again: *"I have told you I will do it. Where is your faith? Do you believe it's going to happen?"*

Jerry did.

"Okay then. Cut off all ties and go."

It was the first time Jerry had ever relinquished his life security. He knew he could lose everything—including his reputation.

But the Roses of Texas packed up and left the South. Headed for the Land of Lincoln. Happy.

---

*William Shakespeare was a prophet: "What's in a name? That which we call a rose/By any other name would smell as sweet."—*Romeo and Juliet.*

Chapter 12

Missionaries Know

Pandemonium greeted Jerry Rose in Chicago. We had finally reached our agreement with the C.F.L. during my trip to Washington. All we had to do was get a license from the F.C.C. within six months, and the station would be ours. Except for one other minor point: we had to produce a million dollars before July 31.

We released a floodtide of publicity. "Congratulations!" our newsletter screamed in big bold headlines. "You bought Channel 38!" The smaller print explained the details.

Jerry arrived to find us frantically scrambling for donations, pumping out publicity, exploding by spurts in dozens of directions at once.

We gave Jerry The Stone Church choir room as an office. He had a big table for a desk. If he needed a telephone, he had to use one of the staff members' offices. Luckily on each day of the week a different staff member had his day off.

Here was the most widely experienced and most highly trained professional we had—and somehow he got struck with the lowliest beginnings.

If the next few weeks had been fiction, no reader would have believed them. Television professional Jerry Rose was about to discover that—in Chicagoland—he was as helpless as Owen Carr. I thought Jerry would be our miracle-worker. He had already put one Christian television station on the air. *He knew how.* Soon my bubble burst. Before long the words of Isaiah 60 would be etched in sweat on Jerry's brow.

Obviously, the first item on Jerry's agenda was finding office space for the station that didn't exist yet. Day after day, as the fall grew cooler and then colder, Jerry walked the sidewalks of the Loop with Ron Dudley, a carpenter who had volunteered to help us until we got on the air.

It was at this early point that Jerry realized all his years of experience had not taught him how to rent office space. It was a function he had never needed before, and now he found himself in the position of student—learning the tough way, by bits and pieces, as he bounced from one office landlord to the next. Leasing terms, square footage—they were all a foreign language.

Jerry proved to be a fast study. Before winter blew in, he knew what he wanted: Twenty North Wacker Drive.

It is one of the great addresses of Chicago, housing the Civic Opera and Civic theatre. From the lake on the east it is a venerable old structure of 1920s architecture, with the uppermost stories recessed in tiers. From the city on the west it is a solid, strong, modern address, emblazoned with the name of the building's owner: The Kemper Insurance Company.

Jerry was taken by the majesty—the Chicagoness—of Twenty North Wacker. It had an elegant old lobby, complete with uniformed doorman. The price of space, Jerry discovered, was right. And the building was just a few steps in either direction from two of the commuter train stations that Chicago relies on so heavily.

The first official office staff consisted of Jerry Rose, vice president and general manager, and Nancy Fabiszak, secretary-bookkeeper. The president of the corporation, such as he was, had no office.

Jerry leased one office, a tiny reception area, and an overgrown closet with shelves that doubled as storage room and counseling center. There was, however, no counseling ministry yet. Jerry already was dreaming and scheming.

In reality our entire scheme was still little more than a dream. But Jerry began cooking at full boil anyway. In a matter of weeks he had laid a groundwork of public and private relations with Christians all over Chicagoland, and indeed all over the country. While nobody was interested in committing any money to buy air time on a station that might never exist, still many of Jerry's Chicago contacts proved to be vital as the months progressed.

It was during this time that Lex Young, still employed by the C.F.L., was drawn more and more deeply into the circle of our ministry. Jay Kessler, national head of Youth For Christ, became our dear friend. Film producer Jim Grant and his wife Myrna of the Wheaton Graduate School of Communications also came to be part of the ministry's family. And there were dozens of others.

During the next weeks, Jerry pushed and pulled and exhausted himself talking with people in marketing, in journalism, in radio and television, in education, in social sciences—in every imaginable field that could possibly rub elbows with Channel 38 in the future.

Meanwhile, I went to Ecuador for a week. I had been asked to minister to the missionaries of Ecuador and Peru, along with their families. On my way I changed flights in Miami, and from the airport I tried yet another series of fruitless telephone calls, trying futilely to raise funds. No one outside Chicago seemed interested in the project, and inside the city not enough were interested to sustain it without help from outside.

I hung up from the last call with a sigh. It would be good to get away for a week and just preach. I had filled myself full of promotion for the time being.

I had never been to South America, and was astonished at its beauty and its poverty.

I stayed in a hotel at the edge of the Pacific Ocean. My bamboo room stood on four-foot stilts. It had no ceiling, only the underside of the hotel roof. I had cold running water at certain times of the day.

Twenty-eight missionaries plus children had gathered at Esmeraldas, Ecuador. They came from high in the Andes Mountains, from deep in the Amazon jungle, from beautiful Quito, from scruffy tropical villages. They were old and young and veterans and rookies.

But they shared a common hunger: for a new touch from

God. Some had gone months without singing a chorus in English. All of them had been immersed in their work for long stretches of time, and now they were ready for a time of spiritual feeding and refreshing.

It was a beautiful week. Their response to the Word was instant and exciting.

Even as I rested from my promotional labors, I realized that each of these missionaries faced that same task over and over, on every trip back to the States. I remembered the final unproductive calls I had made in Miami only days earlier.

"I think I understand how you must feel at times," I told them one day. "You have a burning desire to reach your field for Christ. Then you come home and try to share that burden with us. You travel, preach, unburden your very souls, and we sit there with hard hearts and callous spirits."

I saw several nodding, no doubt amused by the accuracy of the description.

Then, to illuminate how I could share their feelings, I told them a few of my experiences in fund-raising for Channel 38.

I told them how I had talked to a man who gave generously to religious work. When I had finished sharing my burden, he looked at me squarely and said, "I am not going to give you one dime."

I related how I had shared my vision with a close personal friend of mine, the pastor of a well-to-do church in another state, a church with no debts, with thousands of dollars in the bank. I had asked him for a thousand dollars to help us get on the air. I felt sure he would laugh it off and give five times that much.

"If God wants a Christian television station in Chicago," he said off-handedly, "there are enough millionaires up there to do it."

And as I shared with those missionaries the frustration of the years, I began to weep. It had been a grueling five years—as long as one entire missionary term, come to think of it—without seeing nearly enough of the vision fulfilled, with only a fraction of the vision completed.

"So I think," I concluded, "I must know how you feel."

I sat down. But the Holy Spirit was not at rest. Every one of the twenty-eight missionaries was an American, and my burden for Chicago had come to epitomize their own prayers for all of America. They began to weep with me over Chicago. One man stood and prayed in tears. Then another, and still another, and another.

As the Spirit continued to move, one of the men came forward to speak to the rest. At Christmas his family had received a gift of $500 he said. Every member of the household had already decided how to spend the whole amount.

"There were so many things we wanted," he said.

But the money had not been spent yet, he went on, and now he knew why they had held onto it.

"God wants us to give it to help reach Chicago with the Gospel."

A woman spoke with tears streaming down her face.

"My mother died recently," she said, "and I wanted so badly to go back to the States for her funeral—but I couldn't. I want to take the $500 it would have cost and give it to reach Chicago with the Gospel."

Next a young man stood to his feet with his wife.

"Before we came to Peru we worked among the American Indians. The largest relocation center for American Indians is in the Chicago area—there are 40,000 to 50,000 there. We'll give $500 to help reach Indians in Chicago."

Another woman spoke. "We have electricity in our area now," she began. "And I really need a washer and dryer. We've skimped and saved until now we have enough to buy them. We almost ordered them before coming to this retreat, but somehow it slipped by us. I'll give $700 and do without the washer and dryer. I want to see souls saved in Chicago."

When it was over, the twenty-eight missionaries had given almost $6,000. My heart was broken wide open. All of us wept together before the Lord.

It is startling now to think back over what happened that day in Ecuador. In the truest sense I had witnessed missions giving in reverse. It was a strange and wonderful sensation to realize that ministers of the Gospel who had given their whole lives to a foreign people still loved their native land enough to invest in a mission work back home.

Much later, I walked toward my room with Loren Triplett, the man who oversees missionaries in Central and South America for our denomination. I felt ashamed.

"I didn't come out here to take money from missionaries," I said sheepishly. "I came out to try to be a blessing to them. I'm overwhelmed by what they've done."

"That's all right," Loren said with a smile. "Missionaries know what to do with a burden."

His comment locked itself away in my brain and would not go away. Again and again, as I flew over South America and the Gulf of Mexico, the words echoed in my mind.

Slowly the words conceived a sermon in my heart. I would share it with The Stone Church on Sunday morning: "What Do You Do With a Burden?"

Only three things, according to Scripture—cast it on the Lord, carry it yourself, or share it with others.

"Bear ye one another's burdens," Paul wrote to the Galatians, "and so fulfill the law of Christ." It is a law of love. The message was burning bright within me by the time I landed at O'Hare.

On Sunday morning, I told the congregation what had happened at Esmeraldas. I shared with them the sermon God had given me.

The people were deeply moved by God. I watched as the Holy Spirit allowed them to sense the love and concern of their American brothers and sisters in South America.

The Stone Church had already given far more than a fair share toward Channel 38. But this morning the body of believers once again reached out in faith and gave another $50,000 toward Christian television for their city.

On Sunday night one of the couples of the church stopped me.

"Pastor, we cried all the way home this morning," the husband said. "Would you order the best washer and dryer you can get and ship it to that missionary's wife—and then send us the bill?"

Then the future of the project once more screeched to a halt. Our six-month agreement with the C.F.L. was only days away from expiring. We had $25,000 in escrow which the C.F.L. would keep if we couldn't come up with a license from the F.C.C. before the six-month mark.

Between the pounds of paperwork prepared by our attorneys and the helter-skelter fund-raising efforts of everyone connected with the project, we thought we were all ready for the license to be granted. But nothing was happening; we were getting no signals from Washington.

The F.C.C. wanted $400,000 "in our hands"—above our $600,000 letter of credit, which was designated to buy the transmitter—before it would grant a television license. We were still $150,000 short. For all our scurrying and pumping and promoting, our fund-raising efforts had only left us tired and empty.

A week before the deadline, Jerry and I agreed that he would go to Washington and try to wring a miracle out of the United States government.

"Jerry, just between us, what do you think are our chances of getting this money together?" Shirley asked.

Jerry looked at his wife evenly. "At this point, Shirley, only a miracle of God can put this thing together. It's impossible to raise $150,000 in the time we have left. We've tried for months to raise it, and it's just not there."

On Monday morning, Jerry packed his bags and flew to Washington.

Chapter 13

Marching into Jordan

Deadline: Friday, 4:30 p.m. That was when the F.C.C. offices would close. Our C.F.L. contract would expire at one minute past midnight.

Jerry guessed he would spend one or two days in Washington. By then he should know whether it was going to be *do* or *die*. He took two suits with him, a gray and a blue.

On Monday morning he put on the gray one and walked into Mort Berfield's office. It was their first meeting.

"Well, what do you have?" Mort asked.

"I don't have enough," Jerry replied.

"Jerry, I don't see a way in the world you can get that license unless you have the money the F.C.C. wants. That's the criteria. The only thing standing in the way is the money. Unless you have it, you're not going to get the license."

Jerry looked at the Jewish lawyer, and at that moment he felt a surge of faith.

"Mort, the money will come in. I don't have any idea how, but it will be here."

Mort shrugged.

Jerry borrowed Mort's phone and dialed. When I picked up the line in Chicago, Jerry spelled out Mort's assessment word for word.

We were at an impasse. We had knocked on every door we knew to knock on. The money was not available for such a risky proposition as Christian television in a market like Chicago. There was no hope for raising $150,000 in time to process our application and have a license granted all by four-thirty Friday afternoon. The F.C.C. doesn't work that fast; it's a physical impossibility.

As I listened to Jerry's bad news, I flashed back to the day when God emblazoned Deuteronomy 8:18 on my heart: "Remember the Lord thy God: for it is he that giveth thee power to get wealth, that he may establish his covenant."

Once again my attention was riveted to my own weakness and worthlessness. I had no power to raise this money. I told that to the board on the very first day. And now I began to realize that no mere man—not even the knowledgeable and talented Jerry Rose—could do for God what He had already declared He would do for us.

So God would provide. Once again, He would give us the miracle we needed when all of our own efforts were wasted.

I suggested to Jerry that he start calling Christian program producers around the country and ask for contract commitments. "Maybe they will advance us the money," I said.

Meanwhile I would call various pastors and find out how much they would pledge on behalf of their churches. The money would be there too.

It was a bold plan, certainly no less fanatical than anything we had tried to raise money with before. But God kept recalling to my mind the Scriptures that he had first placed there so many long months before.

"Fear not," He said to me once again, "for thou shalt not be put to shame."

I began calling pastors. I wasn't red-faced or shy. The Word of the Lord was backing me up. I was proud to be calling on His behalf.

Jerry, meanwhile, plodded into the hopeless plan. He placed his first call to gospel singer-evangelist Vicki Jamison, and asked her the standard beggar's question: Do you know anybody who has any money available?

Vicki suggested her friend Marvin Gorman, the prominent New Orleans pastor. Jerry hung up and thought about it. In all the months of drumming up customer contacts, he had never once thought of calling Marvin Gorman—the man who had married the Roses. Jerry had known the pastor for a long time. But he had always thought of Gorman's church program as a strictly local segment. The longer Jerry sat and thought, the more he felt that Gorman's program would indeed be good for Chicago. After all, Jerry realized all over again, isn't that the wonder of the Gospel?

He called Gorman. Yes, he would like to air the program on Channel 38 if it ever got on the air. Until that time, Gorman's church would make a loan of $25,000 available if needed.

Jerry hung up, a little surprised. Zero to $25,000 in five minutes is enough to cause emotional whiplash.

But Jerry dialed on. He called Gerald Derstine, founder of the ongoing Christian Retreat in Bradenton, Florida. Gerald was willing to buy about $21,000 worth of air time. Consider it sold.

Then Jerry contacted Word of Life, Jack Wyrtzen's group headquartered in Schroon Lake, New York. They bought a half-hour time slot.

And so on!

Jerry was almost alarmed at what happened in the space of an afternoon. When we totaled the calls that day and the next, our commitments came to $175,000.

It was barely believable. God had directly and divinely intervened. "Thou shalt not be ashamed . . ."

Wednesday morning Jerry walked into Mort's office and announced, "We've got it. In fact, we've got $25,000 more than we need."

It was a good thing. The F.C.C. does not usually accept 100 percent of a group's pledges and program contracts. But what we had was all we had to offer. Mort would try to make it fly.

All Wednesday morning Mort slaved over the paperwork that would get us through the door at the F.C.C. Before noon Jerry and Mort were sitting in conference with Roy Stewart of the F.C.C. and one of the agency's accountants.

The accountant flipped through the contracts and pledges one by one.

"We can't accept this."

"Why not?" Roy asked. "It looks okay to me."

"Well, okay, I think we can accept it."

Jerry watched the two men repeat the process again and again. It seemed that Roy Stewart, an employee of the federal government, was playing the role of advocate for Christian television in Chicagoland—something Jerry never expected to see. The Holy Spirit was quietly at work in the room.

By the end of the conference the F.C.C. had accepted every contract and almost every pledge—well over $150,000 worth had been okayed by the accountant.

"*Good,*" Jerry thought. "*Now if we can just squeeze the two-week processing schedule down into two days . . .*"

But with five years of frustration already invested, Satan was not going to bow out gracefully now. Now he began to rail at us, to taunt us with a devilish sort of sarcasm.

The F.C.C. man who processes license applications was out of the office—on jury duty—when they called.

"*Jury duty!*" Jerry exploded. "What do you mean, jury duty? The Federal Communications Commission shouldn't have to do jury duty!"

He was furious. It was so idiotic.

"Especially when something this important is pending!" he went on. "You know we're right down to the wire on this thing, and you tell me jury duty!"

"That's right," Mort replied quietly. "They call the shots."

Jerry shook his head. "This just blows my mind," he sighed.

"That's the way it is," Mort said with a shrug.

When would the man be back in the office?

Hard telling.

Jerry watched as Wednesday evaporated.

It has always been that last-ditch, all-or-nothing, live-or-die, sink-or-swim act of faith that has brought about God's great miracles. The Israelite priests must have looked silly—and felt worse—as they marched down the banks of the Jordan River. But God had said the Jordan would stop flowing when the priests' feet touched the water—and that extreme action, foolish as it seemed, was all it took for God to act.

That same foolish faith was to bring victory out of madness in Washington.

Jerry was wearing the blue suit again—open at the collar this time, though—as he walked into a cloud of tension at Mort's office on Thursday. It was less than thirty-two hours from the deadline.

"Jerry, the last time I talked to Roy Stewart he was pretty upset."

Jerry held his thoughts at bay.

"He feels we're pushing the F.C.C., and he really won't tolerate that."

Jerry remained silent.

"What we're going to have to do is back off, wait and see what's going to happen."

Jerry bit his tongue.

"It looks like nothing is going to happen until at least 4:30 p.m. today. They said as soon as they could get something done they would call me."

Jerry looked at Mort. He felt his hands being tied before him. He had no recourse. It was the F.C.C. The government.

"Okay. Well, I'm going to go, then."

Jerry stepped out of the office and onto the streets of the capital.

"Lord, it's in Your hands," Jerry prayed silently as he walked. "You're going to have to do it. I know You've ordained this project. I've done all I can. It's entirely Yours. I'm confident that You're going to put this thing together."

The words of Isaiah 60 tumbled through Jerry's mind all over again.

"The sun shall no more be thy light . . . but the Lord shall be unto thee an everlasting light . . ."

God would do it Himself. That's how He wanted it.

Jerry spent Thursday playing tourist. He saw the Smithsonian Institution and the National Archives and enjoyed himself immensely.

Every couple hours he checked in with Mort by phone.

"Nothing, Jerry," Mort always replied. "I don't have any word at all."

Once Jerry suggested that Mort take the initiative.

"I just don't think I can call them back," Mort said.

The Day came.

Friday morning found the future of Christian television in Chicagoland huddled in a time corner, squeezed into a now-or-never situation. By all indications, the project was going to suffocate right here.

"What have you got?" Jerry asked as he walked into Mort's office wearing a slightly rumpled gray suit.

"Nothing." Mort hadn't heard a word.

He placed a call to the F.C.C. He hung up. They were working on it, they said. They couldn't guarantee anything, but they were working on it.

Jerry sat around the office all morning. At noon, he and Mort went out to lunch. After lunch Jerry was tired of sitting around the office. So he walked around the office. After a while he had visited all the corners of the office, so he began to stalk the building itself. To this day he does not remember where he went.

But Jerry came back at 2:35 p.m. Mort had an odd, almost quizzical look on his face as he handed Jerry a little blue "while-you-were-out" note.

Jerry burst into waves of laughter. "This has got to be the understatement of the century!"

Mort stared at him, somewhat cautiously. Then Jerry phoned me.

Like a cat delighted with the capture of a mouse, Jerry had to play a game.

"Well!" he sighed into the telephone.

He didn't go on.

"Have you heard anything?" I asked him. I believe I was trying to sound stoic, but I had been sitting at the phone literally all day.

"Yes, Owen," he replied evenly. "We've gotten word."

"Well?" I wanted to know. "What was it?" My mind in that moment was a void, waiting to be filled with only one of two possible responses. In that flash of time, I didn't know which I really expected to hear.

On the other end, Mort couldn't believe what he saw Jerry doing. Suddenly he grabbed the phone and shouted, "We got it! We got it!"

"Yes," Jerry said. "We've got it."

I sat silent, awed, struck to my soul by the gargantuan realization of it. *"Chicago has been granted."* What an understatement indeed! The thought was left unfinished—Chicago has been granted Christian television! Chicago has been granted an alternative! Chicago has been granted a miracle—maybe unlike any other in her history! Chicago has been granted a blessing so immense that none can comprehend its future!

Chicago has been granted. How perfectly true.

Owen Carr had not been granted anything. Jerry Rose had not been granted anything. No person, no preacher, no religious group had been lionized by this event. Chicago—the City—the Metropolis by the Lake—the millions of souls within her reach—had been granted.

So God *did* love the city. He had proved it by pulling our flimsy human plans out of the fire, then tossing them away entirely and consuming the fire Himself. Less than two hours before the deadline—in the slice of time where no human power could make any difference anymore—God stretched forth His hand and intervened on behalf of Chicagoland.

God loved the city. "Chicago has been granted." Ah, those old tears of compassion welled up in my eyes once again.

Jerry waited a long time on the other end of the line for my response. I had no elegant words to quote for posterity. I could only give credit where credit was clearly due.

"Praise the Lord," I said quietly.

When I hung up the phone, I immediately closed the church offices, and the staff and I had a prayer meeting in the sanctuary. It was a grand and beautiful time we spent worshiping Almighty God. The Spirit of the Lord was present in a very close and personal way. It would have been a lovely closing chapter to the story of Channel 38.

But nip was never very far from tuck.

Chapter 14

As Good As Dead

Almost before we could catch our collective breath, our greatest trouble yet was facing us. Suddenly Martin Ozinga had called and blown down our $600,000 house of cards.

In one wretched evening, we had nosedived into oblivion—as low a point as we had ever been—and deeply committed to public ridicule besides, for all the publicity we had already released.

As could almost be expected, we had been tripped up on the only single clause in our agreement with the C.F.L. that had yet to be satisfied: We had to close the deal with the C.F.L. within two weeks of getting our license.

And now, with Martin Ozinga refusing to let go of the $600,000 on the eve of the deadline, even that simple clause in the contract became an Everest—an insurmountable mountain to conquer or be conquered by.

We humans had done all the human things we could do. At one point during the long, long board meeting, I had even called Paul Crouch, who had successfully pioneered Christian television in California. I hoped he would take the desperate hint and offer to underwrite us. But instead he assured me of his prayers. I knew, sadly, it was all he would do.

Our options had dwindled. The board had met and prayed—I wondered how many were praying silently for mercy, having written off the outcome as a total disaster—and we had talked, cajoled, and reasoned until all reason was exhausted.

Martin Ozinga called once more after everyone else had left the church. My hopes soared, then skidded to a stop.

"Reverend, I hope you don't think I'm trying to get out of an agreement with you."

I paused to consider that question, unsure of what my answer would be. I only knew this: if there is one bank in the country where your money is safe, it is the First National Bank of Evergreen Park.

"But this is why we have attorneys," he said. "I cannot go against my legal counsel. I hope you understand."

He was kind, but very firm. I thanked him and said goodbye.

It was already in God's hands.

Ironically, I had put together a sermon that week called "God Is Just Waiting For You to Die." I looked at Abraham, who was a hundred years old—as good as dead—before God fulfilled His promise of a son. I considered Isaac, stretched upon an altar as a human sacrifice. Isaac was as good as dead when God began to use him. I recalled Jacob, who ran from his murderous brother, falsely accused by his master's wife, unjustly imprisoned for nine years, forgotten by the man who could have saved him.

Joseph was as good as dead for twenty-two years—more than half his life—before God began to use him.

Moses, also, and Peter as well, and Paul the apostle, and Jesus Christ the Son of God—all these were as good as dead, but God delivered each one and used them through that death. God was just waiting for them to die.

We think death follows life. God thinks differently. "Except a corn of wheat fall into the ground and die, it abides alone. But if it die, it bringeth forth much fruit" (John 12:24). God's principle is that life follows death.

As I drove home from the board meeting, I thought through that sermon again. Suddenly it felt a little too timely for me.

But above all things I believed this: God's Word is true. And if God was just waiting for us to die before He could really begin using us, then I had only one prayer left to pray:

"Lord, please use us before they bury us."

I came home from the long board meeting and checked on Priscilla. She was less frantic now, sleeping fitfully. She was exhausted after the news that our granddaughter Nicole had stopped breathing and had been rushed to the hospital.

By now, I thought, all the board members must be home, shaking their heads and spelling out the tragedy of the television project for their sleepy wives.

But I was content. I had followed God's leading as best I could for well over five years. Now, if God had fulfilled His will and was shutting down the project, I was prepared to accept that.

The trumpeting press releases were already lying on editors' desks and newscasters' copy stands all over Chicago.

"Not many wise . . ."

Tomorrow, when the banker showed up empty-handed at the C.F.L. office, I would indeed become perhaps the greatest fool the city had ever laughed at.

". . . That no flesh should glory in his presence."

No danger of that right now.

It was nearly midnight when I crawled into bed; I did not hear the clock strike the hour. I was at peace.

Not far from the parsonage lived Bob Honig, one of Ozinga's vice presidents. The two men had been in touch during the evening.

Bob Honig was in bed by 11:45 p.m. He heard his clock strike midnight. Also one o'clock. And then two o'clock.

Like Daniel, I slept in the lion's den—while the king was up all night.

The day began well. Our daughter called from Cincinnati: our granddaughter Nicole had passed the crisis point. She would live to be a healthy young lady.

I arose as usual at 5 a.m. and got ready to go downtown. I left the house, made a few stops to collect some necessary paperwork, and headed down to the C.F.L's Marina City offices.

Jerry Rose woke up with the same odd sense of well-being that morning. He stopped off at his office before coming to the meeting. As he walked into the lobby at Twenty North

Wacker, he was taking stock of the situation.

"I really should be panicky right now," he said to himself. "But I'm not."

"Maybe I'm underestimating the whole thing," he reasoned. "Maybe if I knew how bad it really is, I wouldn't feel so peaceful."

But it was a peace past understanding, and it could not be shaken off or driven away. There was absolutely nothing in the natural to foster it—Jerry knew that perhaps better than anybody—but the calm had settled in, regardless.

"The sun will no more be thy light . . ."

Jerry recalled God's direction in Virginia: *"You are going to Chicago. And when you go . . . it's going to be so far beyond what you are able to accomplish that you're just going to have to relax and trust Me and let Me do it My way."*

Apparently God was still firmly in control—somehow.

I arrived at 10:30 a.m. I did not want to be late for my own funeral, if that was what this was to be.

Jerry and our other board members arrived. Our local attorney, John Hanson, arrived. We were all seated in a little side chamber, while the C.F.L. officials gathered in their main conference room.

At eleven o'clock, the C.F.L. president's secretary informed us that our bankers had called. They would be late.

Hanson drummed his fingers on the table. Twenty minutes passed. Jerry tried to kick around some alternatives. There were none to kick around anymore.

At 11:30 a.m., the grim became ridiculous. We were $600,000 short, without a banker, and late for a meeting with the Chicago Federation of Labor. It was as true a limbo as I have ever been suspended in.

At 11:45 a.m. we were notified that Kenneth Ozinga, Martin's son and assistant, and Anthony Le Pore, the bank's attorney, had arrived. They had already joined the C.F.L. officials and other people in the main conference room. I could imagine the lions licking their lips as we appeared in the arena.

When young Ozinga and the attorney walked in, I explained with a final stoicism: "I feel at least we should know where we stand when we go into that meeting." There was a pause.

The attorney spoke up. "We have been in touch with Washington."

Who could tell what that meant at this point?

"We talked to the F.C.C. this morning," he continued, "and we understand that a license and a construction permit are basically the same. We are prepared to go ahead with the loan. We have the money with us."

I looked at Jerry and John and silently mouthed a single word: "Hallelujah." Hanson replied in kind with "Amen."

The vision lived again. It had truly died—we were sitting in the ashes of disaster—when God resurrected the dream. We were as good as dead . . .

We felt like hopping, skipping, and whistling into the conference room, but instead we solemnly filed through the door. As we sat down, I felt no celebrity shock. The lawyers, the officials, the judge—none of them awed me anymore. I was the son of the King; I was doing His business. No man in that meeting could hold back the divine power of my Father, Almighty God.

My exterior was calm, but inside I was having a shouting revival. The other men in that room would never know where I had just been. They would never know my agony of dying, nor the joy of resurrection.

Glory to God! He was just waiting for us to die!

The various attorneys had compiled a checklist fourteen inches long—of matters that required attention before the sale would be official. Some of the items were our responsibility. Some of them our bank was responsible for. Others were the responsibility of the bank where our $25,000 had been placed in escrow. All of these items had been worked out in advance; our hands were clean.

Ironically, it was the formidable C.F.L. who had slipped up. One of the matters they were responsible for—

transferring their twenty year lease on the space in the Hancock where the transmitter sits—had not been taken care of. They lacked a single signature, and the man who could provide it worked out of John Hancock's headquarters in Boston.

The C.F.L. declared that it was only a formality, but our attorney set his jaw. We were not going to let a technicality unravel our whole ministry somewhere down the future path. Furthermore, Kenneth Ozinga tightened his grip on the $600,000 check, unwilling to turn it over for fear it would purchase a transmitter with no place to put it.

Finally, a C.F.L. attorney left the room to call Boston. When he returned he announced that a Mr. Sears in Boston had assured him he would sign the papers as soon as they arrived. So, the attorney suggested, we could proceed with the meeting.

John Hanson wouldn't budge. Ozinga sat tight.

"What if Mr. Sears dies this weekend?" John speculated. No one else had the authority to sign the papers. Who could tell if anyone else in the Hancock organization even knew that Mr. Sears had committed himself to signing them?

Ozinga put his foot down. The whole fourteen-inch checklist would have to be satisfied, he told the group, before he would release the money. He wanted Sears' signature *before* letting go the check.

The meeting disintegrated into several separate caucuses, this time with the psychological advantage clearly in our corner. It was a welcome change.

Eventually we all agreed on the only realistic solution. We recessed the meeting until Monday at 11 a.m. In the meantime the C.F.L. would fly an attorney to Boston to get that single signature on that single piece of paper.

By noon on Monday I had a new appreciation for the old cliche "signed, sealed, and delivered." With the twenty-two personalities reassembled onstage, we had collected two identical stacks of legal documents, one for the C.F.L. and one for us, each nearly two inches thick. Dozens of the pages had been signed first by me, then by C.F.L. President Lee, then sealed with our respective corporate seals by Cecil Swanson of our board and Thomas Faul of the C.F.L. Over and over we repeated the process, as the attorneys inspected each document and stacked it with the rest face-down on the table.

Now it was time for the money. Banker Ozinga sat with his attorney at one end of the long conference table and passed the check to the man next to them. Each man looked at the check and passed it slowly down the line. It was an awesome sight.

As the check came to me, I held it in both hands and stared. A devastating sensation swept through me.

Now what have I done?

I knew in that moment that there was only one man on the planet who was ultimately responsible to pay that money back—a foolish Kansas farmboy named Owen Carr.

I was just about to pass the check on to the next man when the old still, small voice spoke up again:

"You must go with it. Go with that check."

I knew the Lord had spoken to me, but I didn't understand immediately what He was saying. As I passed the check on, though, I knew.

It was not an entirely pleasant experience. It seemed to mean leaving behind a place and a people I had grown to love as my own flesh and blood: The Stone Church. They were the ones who had wept with me, sacrificed with me, held me up continually before God.

But immediately the Lord began to confirm His direction for me. That same day, as Jerry and I sat discussing our next moves, I suggested that he set up certain meetings and take certain steps. He agreed.

"But I'm not the person to set up those meetings," he told me very seriously. "That's the work of the president. My calling is not to administration or public relations. My calling is to television operations and production. That's why I rejected the position of president. That's the position God gave *you*."

Now a new factor was beginning to come into focus. But

only barely. I could not foresee what a decision to leave The Stone Church would do to my lifestyle. I could not foresee the financial setbacks, the emotional eruption, the spiritual warfare that lay ahead. I could foresee neither the heights of glory nor the depths of despair that were the future.

Nor could I see, on that victorious day, how Channel 38 might threaten the very foundations of my home.

Chapter 15

Damaged Pieces

Priscilla was my fondest joy in life. In a classic Kansas romance, I had met her at church and—since she lived next door—began walking her home the long way.

Her father had died as the depression was ending. Priscilla and her mother had to move in with Priscilla's older sister, whose husband was pastoring the church my family attended.

Our courtship was no Hollywood spectacular, but it brought two hearts together. We spent Sunday afternoons and evenings together, and sometimes I left the meat block early to spend an hour or two with her on a week night.

One evening as we sat together I suggested she might like to change her name to Mrs. Owen C. Carr. She gave me a shove.

"Sit up and calm yourself," she scolded.

I was not flashy, but I was persistent. The engagement ring was ceremoniously presented to Miss Priscilla Faye Seidner on July 27, 1941. We planned to marry in a year, after I had been graduated from Arkansas City High School.

Suddenly that winter World War II broke loose. Some of my friends quit school to enlist. Every healthy male was a candidate for war. I might be gone by time for the wedding.

Money was good at the frozen foods plant. I was making more money than my father. I could support a wife, and I had already chosen one. With the future so uncertain, Priscilla and I decided to move up the wedding date—to New Year's Day, 1942.

Eight people stood near an old wood stove while a freezing

blizzard raged outside. Sometimes the ceremony still strikes us funny. When Priscilla said, "I do," her nervous voice cracked a little. So when it was my turn, I bellowed out a loud and strong, "*I do!*"

I was a disappointment to Mother Seidner. She had prayed for years that her three daughters would marry ministers. The oldest married an evangelist, and was an excellent preacher in her own right. The middle daughter married my pastor in Arkansas City.

Priscilla, the youngest, married a meat-cutter.

Less than ninety days later, I told my new bride that I had been called into the ministry. Priscilla was beautiful. She pledged her loyalty and faithfulness to me and to the ministry God would give me.

It proved to be a grueling pledge to keep.

For nine years we lived in drafty, stuffy, too-hot, too-cold, too-small houses. The well-off butcher who could have been was now a threadbare preacher who had to decide each week whether to pay his bills or buy groceries for his family. Our clothes were rags. Our furniture was junk.

Ah, but Priscilla was beautiful. She made life a pleasant stroll for me. Our home was a cheerful place to live.

She became a master of making ends meet. She sewed her own clothes. Keeping me comfortable became her craft. She did not complain.

Priscilla was a gem.

Mom Seidner moved in with us to be on hand for the arrival of our firstborn. Mom Seidner was a true saint of God, deeply led by the Word. Although she was mild and soft-spoken, she had preached in her younger days, and now she truly blessed our home.

One evening as I came home from work, Priscilla said, "Honey, I think this may be the time I need to go to the hospital." The hospital was seventeen miles away.

"Well, I'll see about it," I teased her. "If I get around to it, maybe I'll take you tonight."

Mom Seidner's eyes flared.

"You *will* take her," she nearly roared at me, "whenever I *tell* you to!"

Quite soon we were at the hospital.

Dawn had barely broken when the doctor held a tiny bundle of life in his hands.

"It's a boy," he reported.

We named him David: *Beloved.* Two months later I turned twenty. Perhaps, I mused, David would make me a grandfather before I turned forty. (He didn't.) Our second child, Marilyn, was born three years later in Ottawa, Kansas.

Church boards invariably ask a new pastor what his wife does in the church.

"Priscilla is my wife," I always told them. "She is not the church's wife. When I come home from a busy day, I like a warm meal and a comfortable home the same as you do. Priscilla's full-time job is making me happy. If she makes me happy, I will make you a better pastor."

No board ever argued with that.

Priscilla and I had an unwritten and unspoken understanding. I pastored the church. She kept the house. But her part went beyond housekeeping—far beyond. She became the economist of the family, the realist, the pragmatist. She didn't need to be a dreamer because she married one. With a few serious questions she could usually disarm any crazy schemes I concocted.

She was the frugal force, the stabilizing force I needed. But she always, without fail, supported me.

Whenever it came time to make a change in the ministry, Priscilla left the decision to me.

"Wherever God sends you," she told me each time, "I want you to go. And I'll go with you."

For five and a half years Priscilla and I had both looked forward to the day when Christian television would be on its way, and we could once again lead our normal pastor-and-wife life. When I told her God had called me into full-time television work, the realistic Priscilla began to ask some questions—frightened questions.

I was fifty-two years old, with no experience whatsoever in

108

television. My entire ministry—thirty-five years' worth— had come from behind a pulpit. Now I was leaving it all for something totally foreign and altogether too risky.

The Stone Church had provided well for us. The parsonage was spacious, the most beautiful home we had ever lived in. The church provided us cars and picked up all the parsonage expenses. I did not own an automobile, a washer or dryer, a lawnmower, a garden hose, or a snow shovel.

It was up to the television board to elect me to the president's post full-time. I waited outside during the discussion and the vote. Then they called me in. They had elected me president and determined my salary.

That evening Priscilla and I sat at the kitchen table and tried to figure out a new budget. We would have to find a place to live, a car to drive, appliances to keep house. Our new salary measured up poorly against our new needs. Over and over I listed the figures. They would not change. We were either short on income or long on bills. Five hundred dollars short every month. Priscilla looked tense.

Finally I put down the pencil.

"Honey, we started into the ministry more than thirty years ago by faith," I said to her softly. "We are back to that point. We're just going to have to step out in faith and believe God to provide both for the ministry and for us."*

The experts will tell you that a woman generally has a different primary need in each decade of her life. In her fifties, a woman primarily needs security. I had yanked Priscilla's security out from under her.

She began to spend hours weeping.

Realtors laughed at me when I told them how much I

---

*I was surprised to learn later that, at the time, many people thought I had taken The Stone Church for a merry little ride. A young man from a neighboring church told me, "When I heard you had resigned at Stone, I thought, 'Boy, Carr's used that church to get himself into the big-money world of TV. I wonder how much he's making.' I really had it wrong, and I apologize."

could put down on a house. I might be able to get an empty lot for that amount, they said. Finally I had to borrow a down payment. Then we had to wait three months to occupy the house. In the meantime, a new pastor moved into the parsonage, so Priscilla and I stored our furniture and moved in with a niece and her husband in Hammond, Indiana.

Now I had neither an office nor a house. We lived out of suitcases and boxes through a long, hot summer. I began to see the uncertainty growing in Priscilla's eyes. It began to wring her out day after day.

God was certainly faithful to meet our needs—often in surprising ways. The Stone Church bade us farewell with a love gift of $4,000. The church's young people bought us a washer and dryer. Rogers Chevrolet in Rantoul, Illinois, sold cars to ministers for $100 down. With each new blessing, I recalled the Psalmist's testimony: "God hath done great things for us whereof we are glad."

But the move was taking its toll on Priscilla. God had not given her the vision of Christian television for Chicago. The vision was mine. In her quiet way, Priscilla had supported me at every stage of the project—as long as I was still the pastor.

But she could not understand this bizarre turn of events. She felt her husband was leaving the ministry that God had entrusted to him. He was leaving his pastorate to become a businessman, a television executive.

She believed no one would ever ask me to speak again. "Who wants to listen to a television executive preach?" she would say.

Finally, it was time to move into our house. Perhaps this will brighten her spirits, I told myself. The movers came. Eagerly we watched them bring in the first piece of furniture. It was damaged. The second piece also. By the time the sixth damaged piece came through the door, Priscilla was in tears. We had never had much in the way of furniture until after our children were married. Then we had saved and bought some nicer pieces—not fancy, but furniture that would last until we retired. Now it was ruined.

110

I stopped the movers and called their central office. The manager told me to let the men unload the rest, and he would send out an adjuster. Weeks later the furniture was repaired. But the psychological damage was already done, and irreparable. Priscilla had been shattered.

The pioneering days were upon us once again. All the people involved in the television project—Jerry, Dan Wilson, Lex, me, all of us—were forced to spend more and more time away from our families.

It was the worst thing that could have happened to Priscilla at this time. Days and nights she sat alone at home. The zest for life slowly drained out of her.

One day I returned home from a business trip of several days and took Priscilla out to eat at a restaurant. I longed to see her spirits rise. In the middle of the meal she looked at me with an expression of puzzlement and alarm.

"I can feel my heart beating on the back of this chair," she said evenly. Her eyes grew wider. "I'm going to pass out," she said. "I really am."

I felt her pulse. It was racing, fast and hard. A nurse in the emergency ward clocked her pulse at 172 beats per minute, alarmingly high.

Two days later, Priscilla was stricken again. She spent eight days in the hospital undergoing extensive tests. They sent her away with a prescription for some medicine.

The ministry was struggling. The office was a pressure-cooker. Some knew Priscilla wasn't feeling well. None knew that my home had become its own terrible sort of pressure-cooker too.

My priorities as husband and minister had hung suspended in a delicate balance for thirty-five years. If I ever had to choose between Priscilla and the ministry of the Gospel, I would go with the ministry. Both the Old and New Testaments teach that the prophet must put his call above everything else. I knew, of course, that Priscilla would never challenge me in that way. She loved the ministry.

But I also knew if I were forced to choose between Priscilla and any specific ministry, I would choose to cling to my wife. The ministry in its broad sense is a worldwide call. God had already given me a ministry of many facets. I could never insist on one of those facets at the expense of my marriage— although this is the brink where I stood at the moment.

My priority system might be finely tuned and delicately balanced, but the pressure building inside me was about to break loose. Priscilla had begun to neglect the house, a sure sign of emotional decay. Once in a while I took a dust rag to the shelves and sills, or ran a vacuum cleaner over the carpet. All signs of life had disappeared somewhere behind her eyes. The sparkle once there had vanished.

I called Jerry into my office and told him what was happening to Priscilla. It looked like it was going to be impossible for her to adjust to our new life. I would give it a little more time, I told him, but if nothing changed I would leave the work and seek God for another open door.

Jerry gave me deeply needed support at a crucial time. He assured me that he and Shirley would pray in earnest for Priscilla and me. He encouraged me to stay on if I possibly could. In spite of all our problems with the young ministry, Jerry and I had developed an excellent complementary working relationship—neither of us wanted this to end.

Elaine Wilson, my secretary, grew very close to Priscilla during this time, and stood by her in even the bleakest moments.

But Priscilla grew worse.

We made it through spring, and then summer, but tenuously. Priscilla continued to take her medication. It did not help. Little problems loomed huge before her. Inconvenience became tragedy. Priscilla was deteriorating.

I arranged for a brain scan. The doctor read the results and called for a more sophisticated brain test. Priscilla grew frantic—she was convinced she would have to have brain surgery. But the test drew a clean slate. She could keep taking some medicine, perhaps, but there was nothing physically wrong.

It seemed like hundreds of times I told her, softly, "We're

going to make it." She always nodded or failed to respond at all.

Finally one day I said, "Honey, we're going to make it," and she grimaced sharply.

"Don't say that anymore. I'm not going to make it. There is no way out."

The weeks crawled by. My heart grew heavier for my beloved wife. I agonized for her day after day. Half of me was dying at my own hand.

Over and over, the same hopeless question: "Why?" I could never answer her.

Don't we love the Lord?

Yes, we love the Lord.

Are we in His will?

Yes, we are in His will.

Doesn't God love us anymore?

Yes, God loves us still.

When will this end?

I don't know.

How long must I suffer?

I don't know.

Is there any way out?

Yes, there is a way out.

What is it?

I don't know.

Chapter 16

Cancel! Cancel!

We had our construction permit. We had our manager and staff. Now we needed what Jerry Rose called an "origination facility"—a place from which to broadcast our programs.

Millions of cables criss-cross under Chicago. They transport electrical impulses, computerized data signals, telephone conversations, television pictures and sound—all underground. Most of them converge at the great American Telephone and Telegraph building, where cable hookups are housed and monitored by the telephone company. Any cable running into A.T.&T. Central can be connected to any other cable running out. This system was to become the lifeline of Channel 38, as we planned to hook up with the Catholic Television Network of Chicago.

Across the street from our office on Wacker Drive are the studios of the Catholic Television Network, owned and operated by the largest Roman Catholic archdiocese in the world. Through an intricate system of cables and microwave relays, parish houses and Catholic schools all over Chicago can pick up their own network signal.

The Catholic studios alone reportedly cost $2,800,000. They are reputedly the most prestigious studios in the city of Chicago. I believe it. I have seen them.

"I realize it isn't right to be envious," I told one of the network's staff members as I gaped at the beautifully equipped facilities for the first time. "But we can drool, can't we?"

Even before we owned Channel 38, I had talked with the people of the Catholic Television Network about leasing their studios whenever we could get on the air. Later, when

Jerry joined our staff, he too discussed the possibilities with the Catholic Network people—and they seemed excited about the prospect of working with us.

By the time we closed with the C.F.L. we had established a verbal agreement with the Reverend James Moriarty, Chuck Hines, and Doyle Coniff. We would have the telephone company run a cable from our transmitter in the John Hancock under the city to the central A.T.&T. station, and then to the Catholic studios. We would lease the Catholics' equipment and install five phones for our viewers to call if they wanted to talk with our counselors. Our agreement was to last at least three months, then we could renegotiate.

It would have been great to have our own studios and equipment, but we were under pressure to get on the air. The F.C.C. was anxious to have this dark channel activated, so we had agreed to be on the air within four months of purchase. We had also contracted with the C.F.L. to be on the air within that time frame.

We would have needed hundreds of thousands of dollars' worth of equipment to get rolling on our own—cameras, videotape recorders, time-base corrector, an audio board, a film chain. The shopping list goes on and on, and in our tiny organization only Jerry Rose and a select few others knew what all those expensive groceries really were.

We *might* have begun with our own equipment and studios. We expected to. We expected the Christian world of Chicago to rally around us as soon as we had actually sealed the C.F.L. deal. We assumed that our trickling income would splash into a floodtide. We assumed we would be able to buy all the equipment we needed long before the four months were up.

Not so. Giving was at a standstill, with no perceivable increase even after we had the station in our possession. Perhaps some thought the battle was over. It was not. We were still down there on the field, fighting it out.

With three of the four months behind us, Jerry broke some interesting news to me. Even if we suddenly got all the money we needed, it was already too late to buy equipment.

Buying television equipment takes time—from placing the order to delivery to installation—and time was what we were out of.

So it looked like the Catholic Television Network would be our first home. It was hard to complain, with the most sophisticated equipment in the industry right at our inexperienced fingertips.

Jerry (gleefully, I believe) ordered the cable hooked up, and got the Catholics' carpentry shop started on a set that he had designed for our first live program, a talk show called "Chicago." Then he arranged with Lex Young for the installation of the five phone lines.* Jerry had also set up a tentative schedule of programing, and now he ordered all the programs in.

We released publicity announcing Memorial Day, Monday, May 31, 1976, as our first day on the air. We would sign on at 5:30 p.m. What a glorious rallying moment it would be for the Body of Christ in the greater Chicago area!

All systems, in the lingo of the Space Age, were go. Until T-minus six days and counting. That was when God's last-minute miracle plan went into action again.

I was out of town on that last Tuesday of the month when Doyle Coniff of the Catholic Network called Jerry. He wanted Jerry to come over to the network offices. He and Chuck Hines wanted to talk to him.

"Is there a problem?" he asked Doyle on the phone.

"Well, sort of."

Jerry ran across the street to the network offices.

Cardinal Cody, perhaps the most powerful Catholic in the country, he was told, had decided that the Church had more pressing matters—on a national basis—that required the services of the network studios. This local Protestant work would interfere.

---

*Lex was now employed by Christian Communications of Chicagoland, Inc. We bought Lex with the transmitter, almost as if he were part of the equipment. Today he is our chief engineer, one of the most vital links of our operation.

116

It was out of their hands, the men said. The Cardinal had spoken.

"Do you realize," Jerry asked them, "what you've done to me? And to this television station? We were all set to sign on this Monday."

Jerry had to get a grip on himself to begin sorting out the problem rationally. He had Lex cancel the phone lines. He now had a talk-show set on his hands with no studio to put it in. Doyle Coniff agreed to hold it until Jerry could find a place for it. The hook up of the Channel 38 cable to the Catholic Network cable had to be cancelled.

The publicity was already out. No way to cancel it.

When I arrived on Wednesday, Jerry and I immediately headed back to the Catholic Network offices. We talked and cajoled and reasoned—still in good shape after talking and cajoling and reasoning with Martin Ozinga just four months earlier—but neither Moriarty nor Hines would change their position. They would prove to be even less flexible than Ozinga had been.

They couldn't, they insisted. Their orders came from higher up.

We tried desperately to set up an appointment with Cardinal Cody. "Sorry, the Cardinal's calendar is full," we were told.

It wouldn't help anyway, Moriarty and Hines shrugged. The decision is final. It's useless to talk.

"Dying daily" became a grim reality for me in those next wretched days. I could see the dream washing away. What could I *do*? Like young Joseph, I sat bewildered in a foreign land.

I looked at that Old Testament character, and I suddenly realized that God didn't expect me to *do* anything at all. Joseph was as helpless and ignorant as I was. He was plucked out of his homeland and imprisoned in a place he knew nothing about—all as part of God's plan! Everything he would learn about righteousness he had already learned. He could do nothing to change his situation.

He had every reason to grow bitter. He had been dealt a

mean hand. But Joseph hit upon that universal formula of faithfulness. In spite of the bad deal, he kept his heart right before God. Joseph was simply what God wanted him to be, where God wanted him to be. It was on that helpless and ignorant foundation that God *taught* him what He wanted him to *know* and helped him *do* what He wanted him to *do*. Knowing things and doing things were not Joseph's responsibility as he sat in that prison—only *being* God's man in God's place at God's time.

Joseph was not unique in his helplessness and ignorance, I realized. With the Catholic studio rug pulled out from under us, we were reduced to the same position. Once again, suddenly, we were a bare-bones operation, filling out God's will in the simplest, most helpless way. We did plunge into a frenzy of agitated activity that week. But we might as well have sat on our hands, watching the clock and the calendar, for all we accomplished.

Even skid row denied us. We investigated a production studio on the fringes of the ghetto, but it wasn't equipped for direct broadcast. It only furnished productions for advertisers—grocery store commercials and the like.

"Fear not; for thou shalt not be ashamed..."

Friday dawned. It seemed impossible to believe those words of Scripture. We had less than a hundred hours to put a television station on the air in Chicago. We had no studios. Even if we had studios, we had no equipment. Even if we had equipment, we had no cable to link the studio equipment to our Hancock cable at A.T.&T. Central. Even if we had a cable, we had our talk-show set standing in the Catholic carpentry shop, waiting to be shipped out.

"Neither be thou confounded..."

They were impossible, even silly words in the perspective of the moment. I was indeed confounded. Even Jerry was exasperated. He had spent the sum total of his wide experience.

Jerry and I made a final futile attempt—we arranged to meet with Bill Brackett and Bob Ford of Olympic Studios. These men had contacted us long before about leasing their studios to us—back when we had no need for them because we were cozily looking forward to the luxurious Catholic facilities.

The appointment was set for 2 p.m. Three days and three hours before air time. Meanwhile Jerry called A.T.&T. in a spurt of faith and asked them to hook our cable into the Olympic Studios line.

"Sorry, sir, but Olympic doesn't have a cable."

"Well, then, install one at our expense."

"Sorry, sir, but that's a two-day job."

"Fine. We need it operating by Monday."

"Sorry, sir, but Saturday and Sunday are not working days, and Monday is Memorial Day, sir. That's a holiday."

"I know Memorial Day's a holiday."

"We'll send someone out to check on it next week for you, sir."

"I need someone today."

"I'm sorry, sir, but I don't see any need for a man to come out today, since we won't be able to do any work until next week anyway."

"But I need you to send a man today."

"I beg your pardon, sir, but as I said—"

"I need a man here today. Right now."

"I—perhaps I could send a man over, just to check on the situation."

"Thank you. I'll expect him in an hour."

Jerry and Lex and I sat down with Brackett and Ford at 2 p.m. At first the men from Olympic were excited about taking us on as a client. "How soon do you want to go on the air?" they asked.

"Monday."

Brackett and Ford looked at us blankly for a moment. Then they looked at each other, but no less blankly. They were taking on crazies as clients.

"Okay," Brackett said with a shrug. "Let's work it out."

Working it out was a gargantuan understatement of the task before us. Olympic Studios had no cable, Brackett explained first of all. The phone company was clearly not going to install one in time. We might have hooked up a microwave transfer from Olympic to our antenna on the Hancock, but there wasn't time for that either. Furthermore, Olympic had no time-base corrector, a sophisticated piece of equipment that we absolutely had to have to put our programs on the air.

Two men arrived from the telephone company and began rummaging around in the back of the Olympic building. Meanwhile, in the office up front, the five of us negotiated the lease of the studios. The larger problem—getting on the air without cable or time-base corrector—had stumped us all.

Suddenly one of the telephone men stepped into the doorway of the office.

"What's that cable back there?" he asked, thumbing over his shoulder.

Brackett frowned. "I don't have any cable back there," he said.

"All I know is, I opened a box," the telephone man replied, " and there was a cable."

We all jumped up and hurried back through the building. On a wall hung a metal box, like an overgrown fuse box, with the door on the front swung open.

Coming out of the box was a cable.

It begins in a box as four cables, this magnificent conductor of light and sound, and the four converge to become one. This single cable stretches up and out of sight, somewhere in the walls of the building, and then crawls under the city to A.T.&T. Central.

"It has to be dead," Brackett said. "I've owned this business five years, and I never knew that cable was there. But I'm sure it's not live. The man who sold to me either cut all the cables or pulled them out before I moved in. It can't possibly be live."

While we went back to our negotiations in the office, the two men from the telephone company tested the mystery cable. Before long they brought their report.

It was live.

It was hot. It was connected to A.T.&T. Central.

What's more, it was available for live full-color television transmission. Immediately!

A quick call to the telephone company had the Olympic cable hooked up to our own, which ran from Hancock into A.T.&T.

Hallelujah! seemed too mild at the moment. God had provided an incredible, fabulous miracle—true to His Word!

"Neither be thou confounded..."

We may have had a revival right there in the studios, except that we still had one serious problem: no time-base corrector.

Brackett and Ford had already scouted the metropolitan area for one of these rare animals. The only ones in the entire city already belonged to television stations. It was a city of nearly 45,000 retail stores, but not one of them was running a sale on time-base correctors.

I knew less about television equipment companies than anybody in the room, but I suggested a name anyway. It couldn't hurt.

"Call Roscor," I said to Lex.

Brackett and Ford together explained to me that only a big company would have something as expensive as a time-base corrector. The Roscor Company had not even been able to finance our minimum equipment needs back when we thought we might buy our own.

But they hadn't called Roscor at all, and I hated to leave even a too-small stone unturned. Finally I talked Lex into calling them.

While our talks continued, Lex left the room to place the silly call. Five minutes later he was standing in the doorway.

"Do you want it tonight or in the morning?" he asked.

Olympic picked it up that night and installed it the next morning.

Had it been fiction I would have written it off as too unbelievable. But once again God had intervened. This was His project; He was putting it together, clearly and completely.

It was entirely out of our fumbling hands.

Now the proverbial monkey jumped to Jerry and Lex's back. With cable and time-base corrector in hand, they would have to put the station on the air in seventy-two hours—something that both of them knew was impossible regardless of the cable and the time-base corrector.

Jerry and Lex asked me to step into a separate room with them. Then they talked; I listened.

Carefully they explained to me every detail of the dilemma. We still lacked dozens of the things we should have had by now to get on the air by Monday. Because of their expertise in the world of television, they were terrified by the scope of the disaster we were about to create. They recommended that we postpone the starting date and then regroup. But they turned to me for that final decision.

I realized then why God had placed me in the position of president. He had entrusted the burden to me alone; no other person, no matter how perfect for the spot, could duplicate what God had chosen to brand on my heart.

Jerry faced me with utter despair in his eyes. There was no hope. There was not even any hope of finding hope. He was willing to back out—it was the only gap between us. And God had prepared for it even from the beginning. The project was not going to stall out here.

The words of Isaiah rang out in my heart: "My thoughts are not your thoughts, neither are your ways my ways, saith the Lord."

We could find some slides, perhaps, I thought, and run them through our transmitter. We could talk through a microphone and explain where we were and why we weren't broadcasting as we should. Anything to get on the air on time—anything to fulfill the vision that God had locked into my consciousness.

I looked at the tired men. Somehow God rejuvenated my faith in those tense, silent moments.

"We are going on the air Monday evening," I told them, "at 5:30 p.m. as scheduled."

Jerry's face registered weary amazement.

"All right, Owen," he said in disgust. "I'll run the tape

through your teeth and let them watch it in your eyes.''

Inside Jerry was crying out in desperation: "Lord, he just doesn't *understand,* does he?''

I didn't understand a single thing. Ignorant as Moses, and headed for the Promised Land.

Chapter 17

Holiday Weekend

The long, long weekend began with a jolt. Olympic Studios did not have a production crew for on-air television, so they scurried to assemble one. The "Chicago" set was trucked over from the Catholic shop. Jerry and Lex, along with Brackett and Ford, threw themselves into a seventy-two hour chaos marathon, pulling together in one holiday weekend what should have taken the full four months we originally scheduled.

I have watched very little television in my life. I have read even less about its inner workings. I was the president of a station only hours from going on the air and I barely knew audio from video. I could not have known what Jerry and the crew were going through.

I did not even visit the studios until Monday afternoon. I came with Priscilla, happy to see her a little excited about getting the station on the air.

But I expected a television studio to be run something like a business meeting or, at worst, a classroom. Instead I found total confusion. Crewmen were shoving equipment, tugging cables, rolling sets, running back and across and back again. There were shouts and disagreements and grim faces.

It seemed obvious to me that we were not going to be on the air at 5:30 p.m.

Then friends began to arrive. I didn't know better than to invite a crowd to witness the first broadcast in person. The already crowded studios were soon crammed with gawking guests: our banker, Martin Ozinga, Jr., and his wife; our board members and their wives; the television staff members and their companions; our telephone counselors and their companions; a number of pastors and their wives—more than 120 in all.

The crew got more frustrated by the moment, as more and more guests tripped on cables, bumped machinery and generally got in the way of progress. Tempers flashed and flared. I had made working conditions impossible for the crew.

With the minutes ticking off one by one—always just ahead of the crew, it seemed—I took Bible in hand and edged off to one side and watched helplessly.

I had dreamed of this moment, but not in such nightmarish detail. I had envisioned a hushed studio, a softly lit set while the Scriptures were read. But not this.

Jerry and I had agreed that we would devote our very first thirty minutes on the air simply to expressing our gratitude to the Lord for making this ministry possible. We knew we might be broadcasting that first night with a Nielsen rating of zero; but even if God alone was watching, we wanted to go on record with how grateful we were for what He had been able to do in spite of us.

We had laid it out beautifully in our minds. I would sit behind a desk, with an almost invisibly small microphone pinned to my tie, and a big beautiful Bible open before me.

I would begin with Genesis 1:1-3:

"In the beginning God created the heaven and the earth. And the earth was without form, and void; and darkness was upon the face of the deep. And the Spirit of God moved upon the face of the waters. And God said, Let there be light: and there was light."

Through the eye of faith we could see television sets coming on all over Chicagoland. Let there be light, indeed!

Then I would read from Psalm 19:1-3:

"The heavens declare the glory of God; and the firmament sheweth his handiwork. Day unto day uttereth speech, and night unto night sheweth knowledge. There is no speech nor language, where their voice is not heard."

Through the eye of faith we had envisioned the gospel

125

message reaching behind closed doors all over Chicagoland—in the hospitals, the prisons, in the highrises, the ghetto.

And then to Isaiah 9:2:

"The people that walked in darkness have seen a great light: they that dwell in the land of the shadow of death, upon them hath the light shined."

Once more, through the eye of faith we imagined souls converted to Christ before television screens throughout the great city of Chicago.

Then Jerry and I would explain to that first night's audience what this new station was. We would share our purposes, our goals, a little of our amazing, God-led history. Steve McTaggart and Kay Blackwood had come to provide music. And we wanted to spend time just worshiping and praising the Lord on that first glorious evening on the air.

Such a solemn opening seemed unlikely now, as bedlam took over in the studio. It might have been more appropriate to the occasion to come on screaming primal screams, for all the sweat and tension and gritting of teeth going on at the moment.

At 5:25 there was still no break in the frenetic pace, no signal of any kind that air-time would actually happen in five minutes.

About two minutes before 5:30 p.m. one of the crewmen grabbed me by both shoulders, pushed me in front of a set, and barked, "Stand right there!"

He stepped back and looked me over. Apparently whatever he saw suited him. He picked up a hand microphone and thrust it into my empty hand.

"Hold this!" he ordered.

I held up my Bible a little lamely with the other hand.

"What am I supposed to do with this?"

"Hold it!" he barked back.

I held up the microphone.

"Then what am I supposed to do with this?"

"Hold it!" he repeated.

I began to get the picture. No desk. No tie-tack

126

microphone. No softly lighted set. No earthly glories.

The crewman looked me over once more, then stepped back beside a camera. A red light on top of the camera blinked on. He pointed at me abruptly.

"You're on the air!"

The first picture ever aired on Chicago's Channel 38 was the Bible itself, close enough to read the words of Genesis 1:1-3.

A second camera then picked me up trying to hook my finger under the pages of the Bible to turn to Psalm 19. I juggled the microphone and the Bible rather poorly, but awkwardly, haltingly, exhaustedly, we were on the air. But there was an electricity of spirit in that studio that outpowered all the other elements.

Thirty minutes dissolved in no time at all, I discovered that first night. Before we had squeezed in everything we had planned, the half-hour was up and we went to videotaped programing.

At 7:30 p.m. we came back in live with "Chicago," cohosted by Jerry and me. Immediately this local talk-format program became the nightly anchor of the Channel 38 ministry. With our telephone number, 346-3800, flashing across the screen, we opened the program up to the viewers.

It was a timid beginning, compared to my great expectations. No callers were reported being converted the first night. Or the second. But on the third night, someone called in and accepted Christ as Saviour. It was the genesis of a magnificent ongoing ministry of evangelism. Since that night thousands have made Jesus Christ Lord of their lives through the ministry of Channel 38.

I was to learn that pioneering a television station is much like pioneering a church: you start small and stay small, perhaps for a long time. You struggle, you pray, you weep—often and in various sequences.

Indeed, weeping and sacrifice—and the birth pangs of Christian television—had cut deeply into my marriage.

Chapter 18

Firestorm

A mountainous debt began to accumulate in the Olympic Studios account books. Our income was far from matching our need to spend. But Bill Brackett and the people at Olympic were kind, considerate.

"Don't worry about it!" Brackett said whenever I brought up the subject. "We know you're going to make it. We know we'll get our money whenever you get it."

The lax attitude grew more and more astonishing to me as our debt topped the $50,000 mark, and then $75,000, and finally $100,000. But there was no change. They were at ease.

The entire arrangement, in fact, was an easy one. Perhaps we should have learned the value of a written contract in our frantic departure from the Catholic Network studios. But our relationship with Olympic was created overnight, under pressure of deadline, and we never came to the point of signing papers. They trusted us. We trusted them. They put us on the air. We agreed to stay with them at least one year. They agreed to buy any extra equipment needed to produce our programs. We agreed to buy all of that extra equipment back from them whenever we ended our lease—because, after all, we were the only client they had that needed all that stuff. And they agreed to let Lex Young approve each purchase before it was made.

It was a simple, easy-to-breathe-with arrangement. We felt sure we would—and should—be in our own studios by the end of our first year on the air.

The first thrilling year rolled toward its close. We applied for the call letters WCFC—Win Chicagoland For Christ—

one of the earliest of hundreds of suggestions made by our ministry's friends.* In our first year we enjoyed visits to our "Chicago" program by such notables as P.T.L.'s Jim Bakker, Trinity Broadcasting Network's Paul Crouch, singer Big John Hall, and others. Our tiny staff grew to nineteen, and the growing work load still cried for more help. And day after day, souls were saved, bodies were healed, and lives were changed through our young ministry.

Brackett and Ford made an appointment to see Jerry and me to discuss our second year's arrangement. We came into the meeting with a few ideas. We could lease their studios for another year—which we really preferred not to do, since we wanted to be on our own. Or maybe they would sell us their studios. Or perhaps we would simply buy the equipment they had purchased to service our account. We really had nowhere else to go, so we were looking forward to making another very comfortable arrangement with Olympic— buying or leasing or somehow.

Before the discussion was very old, both Jerry and I sensed a change. The men from Olympic seemed to feel threatened by our proposal to buy their studios—or even our proposal to buy the equipment they had asked us to buy a year earlier. The meeting soon grew tense and uncomfortable.

If we would not be staying with them another year, the men indicated briefly, then they would be needing their money shortly. That was certainly logical to me. I made a mental note: we would have to start arranging for that payment pretty soon, one way or another. In the meantime I was more concerned with working out this bigger problem—what to do with Year #2.

---

*Jerry Rose promoted a name-calling contest among our viewers to get the best and most meaningful call letters available. He was going to splash the winner's face and name all over our "Chicago" program and our newsletter. When the hundreds of suggestions were filtered through the F.C.C., only a handful had not already been assigned to some radio or television station in the country. Of the few combinations still available, the board of directors chose WCFC—to Jerry's mixed reactions. His wife Shirley had suggested the name. Jerry sheepishly cancelled the publicity plans. We quietly became WCFC on May 26, 1976.

Nothing was resolved in the meeting. Jerry and I regrouped in our own offices and tried to figure out why the two men had so cornered us on the matters of moving and buying. Moving was something they knew we would consider after the first year. Buying equipment was part of the original agreement. And buying their studios was only a suggestion, not an ultimatum. Why all the pressure?

At the same time Brackett and Ford were asking themselves similar questions about us. Apparently we had made them feel we were pressuring them to sell their entire business to us. Perhaps they considered us a subversive force, having already snatched an entire television station out of the hands of the Chicago Federation of Labor. From that standpoint we might be considered divinely armed and dangerous.

Two weeks later we met again. Our primary question was, Had they changed their position about selling any part of their equipment or operations?

They had not.

The beans slowly began to spill. The Olympic men explained how they felt about our attitude of the previous meeting. The foggy misunderstandings began to clear up. We explained that we had felt the same way about their presentation. Obviously both parties had left the meeting with the wrong impressions.

But, clear skies or no, Olympic Studios was still giving us confusing signals. They stated flatly that, now that they had the needed equipment, they intended to remain a full- production operation. But the last question they asked us was, "If we should sell, how much do you think the equipment is worth?" We said we would make a bid. Jerry and I left, almost shaking our heads with the confusion of it all.

By the end of the troubling conversation we had determined that Channel 38 would definitely be moving out of Olympic Studios by May 30. We would lease space elsewhere and create our own studios.

But we still couldn't see the catastrophe about to crash in on us. So far none of the problems were insoluble.

The next week Tom Sedlacek, president of Olympic Studios, called to arrange an appointment. It was a Monday in March when he sat down in my office with Jerry and me.

"I have a very unpleasant mission today," he said, stern-faced.

I reassured him. "Don't worry about it," I said graciously. I knew our account was in arrears, and that it had been from the beginning. We weren't surprised or upset at all that he was here.

Sedlacek realized that we didn't know why he had come.

"I assure you this is unpleasant for me," he repeated. "But I find it necessary to talk with you very sternly. Your account is overdue by $177,250."

Wrong! my brain flashed back. I had kept almost a penny-by-penny count of our growing bill—besides what our accountant had on paper—and I knew his figure was high by more than $30,000.

But what a trifle compared to the next figure he quoted us.

"Olympic Studios will expect to have full payment within seven days," he said.

I'm sure I blanched. Jerry's eyes narrowed for a moment. To make $177,000 in a week would take an annual income of $9,200,000!

We tried to remain calm and businesslike in the face of the firestorm; but after two long hours of our most specialized activity—talking and cajoling and reasoning, this time with wheedling added—Sedlacek had not budged by a dime or a minute.

Nor would he back down on the incorrect dollar amount. Jerry assured him on his way out that we would double-check our records to be sure of the exact figure.

"I will double-check *my* records," Sedlacek informed us coldly, "since it is *my* records we are going by."

Seven days, $177,250. We could raise $1,000 an hour around the clock for the entire week and still not make the deadline.

In the next numbing hour we checked our books. My memory was correct. Sedlacek had given us a total about

131

$30,000 too high. He soon called to apologize for the error.

It was dubious compensation. The next day a letter arrived by special messenger, requiring the signature of Owen Carr or Jerry Rose for delivery:

"...WCFC Channel 38 is hereby notified that its past due balance of $147,231.55 due Olympic Broadcasting Service through February must be paid in full or that a satisfactory repayment schedule be agreed to on or before 5:00 p.m., Monday, March 14, 1977. Should WCFC fail to meet this responsibility, immediate legal actions will be instigated to protect and collect all monies due Olympic Broadcasting Service.

"...Olympic finds itself in an uncomfortable situation. But because our working agreement is about to terminate, and WCFC's payment history has been one of a consistently increasing delinquency, stern actions are now necessary.

"Because of the joy gained over the last nine months from our working relationship, I trust in your assurances that the past due balance will be quickly paid."

My assurances were assuredly empty ones at the moment. It would take at least two months to secure a loan. We could send out a mass-produced letter, appealing to our tiny mailing list for help, but it would take almost as long to get the pieces printed and mailed as we had to raise the funds. We had no hidden reserves to tap. We had no wealthy benefactor to call. We had nothing.

But I thought once again of young David, facing the giant. "The battle is the Lord's," he declared fearlessly. Perhaps he had already written Psalm 76: "Surely the wrath of man shall praise thee," verse 10 says, "the remainder of wrath shalt thou restrain." David's words became my own as we headed for the firestorm.

I don't pretend that I was passive. I knew we were all in God's hands, but I was anxious about the outcome nonetheless.

With Monday, March 14, the deadline dawned. Jerry woke up and told Shirley, "I wish I could forget about today." It was a rare moment of true unhappiness for Jerry.

"What are we going to do?" he asked me as he sat down in my office. I shrugged. I had no revelation from on high. I had only one very human suggestion: wait until mail time, see what comes in. Then we'll get all our money together, give Olympic everything we have, go on the air and ask the people to supply the need.

It was a weak-kneed suggestion. But since we didn't have the full payment in hand, we would have to cast our hopes upon that merciful phrase in Sedlacek's letter: "a satisfactory repayment schedule."

Nothing special came in the mail. I was a little disappointed. How many evangelists and missionaries had told stories in my hearing about receiving God's provision at the last minute in the mail?

The day wore on. The pressure mounted.

We rummaged through our account books like starved hoboes, picking out dollars as if they were precious crumbs of bread. We found a few. When we scraped it all together, we could put our hands on $17,000.

But our ten-month-old ministry had some other pressing bills to pay—$25,000 at the bank, already past due, and $15,000 in small bills from suppliers.

Perhaps to our Heavenly Father we were an infant organization. To anyone else, we were a very sick baby.

Instead of a letter in the mail, we got a call on the phone. It came at 4 p.m., an hour before our deadline. It was Sedlacek, but he was calling from his attorney's office.

An alarm went off inside me and would not shut off.

Sedlacek talked first. He announced his whereabouts and handed the phone over to Mr. O'Brien, his attorney—which lent a great deal of weight to the message they were relaying.

They had been discussing our delinquent account, O'Brien told me, and he had advised his client to begin immediate legal proceedings to secure the funds.

I could see the headline in my mind's eye: "CHRISTIAN TV SUED; CAN'T PAY BILLS."

Furthermore, O'Brien said, he had also advised Olympic Studios not to sign us on the air that evening.

Not sign us on the air! I cried silently. I looked at my watch. Sign-on was barely an hour away. A different and somehow more tragic headline appeared in my head: "CHANNEL 38 DARK AGAIN."

If they refused to sign us on the air tonight...

In a silent flash, a million words and pictures exploded together in my mind. A question Priscilla asked long, long ago: "How will you face all those people when you've spent their money and you can't get it back?" The compassionate faces of the missionaries in Ecuador, as they emptied their sacrifices onto the altar of Chicagoland. "The City With No Doors." The first moments on the air.

Now the images dissolved to black. The years of labor could be swept away right here, right now. It was not a pleasant picture. In terms of television, it was no picture at all.

"What are you planning to do?" O'Brien asked me.

I hesitated. My impulse was to tell him our plans, to argue the point, to plead with him. But I felt God suddenly light a spark of divine wisdom within me—wisdom beyond human impulse.

I barely created the words I spoke.

"I am surprised to find Mr. Sedlacek already at his attorney's office," I heard myself telling O'Brien calmly. "His letter, after all, said we had until five o'clock to come up with the money or a satisfactory repayment schedule."

We already had part of the money, I told the attorney, not to mention the "satisfactory repayment schedule."

O'Brien wanted to know what the schedule consisted of. God filled my mouth again with the exact words I needed to say.

"At the moment, sir, I am not doing business with you," I told him. "Until five o'clock, we are dealing with Olympic directly."

I told him Jerry and I would be in the Olympic offices in thirty minutes. With money and "satisfactory repayment schedule" in hand.

Chapter 19

Adrenalin Surge

It was 4:15 p.m. when I asked our accountant to draw the check for $17,000. Jerry and I hailed a taxi and headed for Olympic Studios.

Jerry was disturbed. The thought of going on the air and laying out such an exorbitant need made him miserable. He felt the weight of his title—general manager—and wanted to avoid facing his audience with what was sure to be construed as a gross managerial catastrophe.

So we had concocted a new plan, a little less extreme than flinging ourselves on the viewers and begging for the whole $170,000 in a single week. At 4:30 p.m. we laid it out for Sedlacek and Brackett. We would pay $17,000 dollars on the spot and $25,000 a week until our deficit was zero. This would pay them off one week before our first year's agreement was to end.

They did not like it.

With Jerry sitting solemn and silent, I offered Plan B: We would present the need to the viewers on the "Chicago" program at seven o'clock. Then, I told them, we could only wait and "see what God will do."

Sedlacek was not counting on God to pay his bills. He picked up the phone and dialed O'Brien. He wanted the lawyer to stay put in his office. He might need legal advice, Sedlacek said. We had not yet arrived at a "satisfactory repayment schedule."

O'Brien advised him again: "Don't sign them on."

Five o'clock came. A mile to the east, at Twenty North Wacker Drive, our staff turned on a television set to see if

135

our color bars were on the screen on schedule. They were. The staff was momentarily relieved.

In Sedlacek's office, however, we had no television set. Jerry and I had no way of knowing whether or not Channel 38 was dark.

At 5:15 p.m. as usual, a minister came on the air reading Scripture. At 5:30, also on schedule, "Davey and Goliath" rolled onto the screen. Apparently the studio technicians had not been ordered to cancel us. Yet.

Finally Sedlacek asked us how long it would take to raise the funds and have them in hand if we made the appeal over the air. Jerry and I glanced at each other. The door had been cracked open a bit. We jumped through it.

"One week," I offered, without any idea how inaccurate that might be.

Sedlacek sighed and took the $17,000 and okayed the crazy plan.

We tend to read the Bible's heroes-of-the-faith stories with a romantic eye. But I rather believe young David's pulse quickened sharply as he crossed the valley to meet the giant. I expect Daniel to tell me some day that, in spite of his great faith, he experienced adrenalin surge as they lowered him into the lion's den.

Jerry Rose and I likewise experienced adrenalin surge as seven o'clock drew near. We barely knew what to say, let alone how to say it. We had no slick slogans to swear by, no custom-printed envelopes to send out, no computers to tally pledges. In fact we had no time for pledges. We were going to have to ask for cash—now—immediately.

We feared our audience for the first time that night. As the cameras swung toward me, I could not predict the viewers' response. For a moment I expected great support, then in another moment my stomach would turn and I could imagine hate mail and crank calls by the thousands.

Perhaps they would think we had managed their money poorly—why give more now? Perhaps they would think we had waited too long to make some kind of move—how could

136

we explain the intricate inside view of our relationship with Olympic?

"Well, friends, we cut every possible corner, worked with a limited staff when we needed more people..."

"Well, friends, we've tried to maintain as strong a ministry on Channel 38 as we felt God wanted—and that took more money than you, uh, gave..."

Every approach sounded ridiculous.

Soon we would know just how deep or shallow were the loyalties of that invisible audience. The Holy Spirit would either sweep through the city and move the entire body of believers as one—or God would cut us off, having spent enough time and patience on this fumbling ball game.

As seven o'clock neared, I moved in front of the camera. Jerry, stunned, stood deep in the shadows in a corner of the studio. He was staring blankly, not moving.

The "Chicago" program signed on the air without the familiar living room set. Instead, I stood before a makeshift tally board. I felt very small.

With no introduction I began to lay out the situation. I did not hype the drama of it; I had suffered quite enough high drama already. I simply explained that our ministry had a number of outstanding bills, that one of our creditors was demanding payment and threatening to keep us off the air, and that we almost did not sign on tonight because we could not come up with the $170,000 we owed.

That's the amount we needed, I told the viewers. We had not padded the figure in hopes of making 80 percent of our goal—a technique practiced widely in the fund-raising industry. That $170,000, rather, represented the exact amount of our current bills—and the amount we needed immediately to keep the ministry of Channel 38 alive.

"We did not even have time to send out envelopes," I explained. "Just put your gift in one of your own envelopes, address it to us and mail it as fast as you can."

Neither Jerry nor I had in any way prepared ourselves for the tidal wave that struck that night. Even before I had finished explaining the situation, the thirteen phones began jangling. People wanted to help. They wanted to give. They wanted to rescue their television station from a sudden death.

With every new pledge, we praised Almighty God. Soon it was clear that the Holy Spirit was indeed moving mightily through the city, prompting Christians in every part of the metropolis to sacrifice unquestioningly on behalf of Channel 38.

One man had watched the channel for a long time without supporting it. When he heard that someone was threatening to take us off the air, he jumped to his feet and shouted, "They can't do that!" He called in a $100 pledge.

By sign-off time that night our audience had committed $70,000 to the ministry.

Jerry took my hand, his smile gleaming.

"I hated to see you do this," he told me, "but I'm glad you did."

On Tuesday night we opened up our "Chicago" program with a whole new sense of victory. Once again we invited viewers to call in pledges and mail their gifts. By the end of the evening another $40,000 had been promised to the work.

It was on Wednesday that we saw the first fruits of the makeshift telethon. The mail arrived in heaps. We sorted out $34,000 in that single day—far and away a record for the ministry of Christian television for Chicago.

Each night that week the pledges kept coming in, and each morning hundreds of believers marched to the mailboxes. Every day the mail stacked up in our offices: another $34,000 on Thursday, $41,000 on Friday, and on Monday a huge mail sack stuffed with $56,000. Tuesday's mail brought another $14,000.

A total of $180,000 had been pledged; a total of $170,000 actually came in. It was a phenomenal percentage for having done without publicity, or envelopes, or any of the trappings of telethons. It was to become a case study for puzzled fund-raising experts.

"God hath chosen the foolish things of the world," I recalled, "to confound the wise."

God's people in Chicagoland had proved themselves faithful; and the small Channel 38 audience proved solidly loyal.

From the moment the money began flowing in, we began paying bills with celestial delight. First came the bank payment of $25,000. Then came all the smaller bills for suppliers across the city.

And finally, on Wednesday, March 23, the most delightful check of all was drawn and signed. I was already on the road again, speaking at a missions convention in the St. Louis area, trying to get churches to write Channel 38 into their missionary budget.

So Jerry had the privilege of carrying the check to Olympic Studios. Max Ephraim, our board's vice-chairman and a character of impish good humor, could not resist the joy of being present when Jerry handed the check for $147,231.55 to Bill Brackett.

Tom Sedlacek, a little sadly, was not available to receive it.

There was a second harvest—an autumn harvest, if you will—that we reaped as the letters began flooding our offices. Hundreds of people had dropped a letter into their envelopes with their gifts.

"Don't ever get in this far again without letting us know!"

"Let us know when you have needs! . . ."

"We need you. We couldn't live without Channel 38 anymore!. . ."

It was a lavish outpouring of love and concern, a united expression of faith in God and confidence in the ministry of Channel 38.

We shouted and praised God for days and days at Twenty North Wacker Drive. Almost with every letter we began a whole new revival.

And letter by letter, the old dream began to dawn anew. It was the dream of a Christian television station owned by the people of Chicagoland. I saw in those letters what I had hoped and prayed for: the Christians of Chicagoland had come to think of Channel 38 as their own ministry.

God had intervened miraculously, stupendously. He had used the mightiest tool on earth: His people. He had cut across denominational lines and social lines and racial lines and political lines and used as many of His people as were willing to give of themselves on behalf of the city.

The largest single offering of the week was one $5,000 gift. There were a few others of $1,000 or $1,500, or $2,000. But dozens and hundreds and thousands of envelopes had carried only a dollar, or a five, or perhaps a twenty dollar bill. Channel 38 was not claimed exclusively by the people of wealth— although they were included. God had graciously entrusted Channel 38 to the entire body of believers in Chicagoland.

Now that they had accepted the burden, God could go about the business of building the work. Perhaps now, with a little less pressure at the office, I could tend to the snowballing crisis in my home.

Chapter 20

"I Won't Make It"

Priscilla had stopped cooking meals at home. Cooking had been her joy, and no joys were to be left intact in her life.

Her energy was sapped; combing her hair became a chore. A gray cloud of gloom hung about her. She was a shell of the Priscilla Faye Seidner I had wed on New Year's Day in 1942.

Our daughter Marilyn and her family had lived in Kokomo, Indiana, for the past year, and Priscilla and I were able to make frequent visits. Now the children moved to Fort Myers, Florida, and Priscilla slipped into severe depression. They might as well have gone to Africa. Priscilla spent whole days weeping.

I tried to reassure her that she would indeed see Marilyn and David and the grandchildren again. I bought her an airplane ticket to Fort Myers and back. She could leave in early January—right after our 36th anniversary on New Year's Day.

But I knew, painfully, she could never stand to fly alone in her fragile condition—and perhaps, by now, not even with me going along.

It was just before that anniversary, in December of 1977, when she called me into the kitchen. She was straight-faced, her lips set firmly.

On the kitchen counter she had lined up all her bottles of medicine.

"I'm not getting any better," she said evenly. "I'm only getting worse. None of the doctors has found what's wrong. None of the medicine has helped."

I cried out silently to God. "What is she telling me?"

"I'm through," Priscilla said. "I'm not taking any more medicine. God will have to heal me, or I will die."

I took her in my arms and held her.

"This isn't your battle," I told her gently as I held her. "It's ours. We are in this together. Neither of us can understand it, or explain why it has been so long, or why victory hasn't come. But it will come. We will stand together in faith till it comes."

I was working late that night in the office downstairs. It was almost 2 a.m. Priscilla would be long asleep by now.

Suddenly I heard her sobbing behind me. I turned and saw her standing in the doorway, trembling and weeping uncontrollably.

I went to her and put my arms around her.

"I haven't been asleep yet," she cried softly. "I'm not going to make it."

I closed my eyes. They burned hot with tears as I began to pray for my beloved Priscilla. We prayed our way through the night. We prayed our way through the next day. We prayed our way through the next night. Each night she dropped off a little more easily to sleep. Each morning she awoke with a little less death in her face.

Days passed in even tempo. Then an old light began to shine faintly in her eyes. A soft, deep light that I remembered from far away.

She smiled now and again.

One day I came home to find a newly made dress draped over a chair. She had cut it out and sewn it up in an afternoon. It had been two years . . .

I looked around. The carpet had been vacuumed. The house had been cleaned.

A few days later I heard her laugh. I took her in my arms. It was the first time in months I had heard the music of her laughter.

When a teacher faces his class, he identifies the textbook

to be studied. Then he assigns certain pages to be read. The material is discussed in class. Finally he gives the students a test, to see how much they have learned.

God's teaching method is altogether different. He gives the test first. We don't even know what subject we're studying. After the test, the Lord stands beside us, pointing back over our experiences. "Here," He says, "is the lesson I wanted you to learn."

Earthly teachers could never make it work. But God's system stamps the lessons of life indelibly on our hearts. It's tough on the student, but the learning lasts a lifetime.

Chicago became a classroom almost every day for all the "students" in the Christian television project. I learned volumes as the Master Teacher kindly showed me my mistakes. Jerry learned in the same schoolroom—more than he ever thought there was left to learn. The board members, the staff—every person touched by the vision—learned something of the character of God. Of His love. Of His power. Of His mercy.

Priscilla may have learned more deeply than anyone else. Every lesson was a painful one.

But on Friday, January 6, 1978, I put her on a flight to Fort Myers—alone. She landed in fine form and enjoyed her vacation thoroughly. When I called later on, Marilyn answered the phone.

"How's Mother?" I asked.

"I may be a wreck," Marilyn laughed, "but Mother is doing great!"

That night I briefly told the "Chicago" audience about Priscilla's long battle and the beautiful victory God was giving. The phones began to ring immediately, and that week the mail piled high. People responded to that story: they could identify with it.

Many people are hurting today. Some are in the classroom, and the test is tough. Many are struggling, wondering if they are going to make it.

Our Lord says, "Yes, you can make it. You can because I did, and I am the way, the truth, and the life."

Are the battles over? No. Every day presents new conflicts.

Does Priscilla still have struggles? Yes. New pains, new uncertainties, new confrontations. But God is our victory in every battle.

Priscilla has begun to travel with me often, something she never thought she would enjoy. She is meeting new people, enjoying the ministry, and once again filling that place I so totally depend on her to fill.

Every day I thank God. It is so good to have her back.

* * *

Neither were the battles over at Channel 38.

"If you're going to start, " I remembered my dad telling me, "then don't ever stop! And if you're going to stop, then don't ever start!" He could not have known how complex that simple order would become.

Now that we were ending our agreement with Olympic, we had to find our own studios. This looked easy on the surface. We leased the old original American Broadcasting Company (A.B.C.) studios on the 44th floor of Twenty North Wacker.

But studios are only empty space until they are stocked with all the equipment. This was not so easy. Even a basic television studio package would cost hundreds of thousands. Even a small down payment and installation charges would come to $54,000.

So, almost needless to say, we could not order any equipment.

But the need was there, and pressing us. The date was drawing closer when we would have to be on our own. I prayed continually about the need—I knew Jerry was feeling more and more pressure as the cut-off date at Olympic Studios drew closer.

Finally the Lord showed me that, as a ministry is born in faith and sustained in faith, it must also progress in faith. The faith-walk never ceases for the laborers in God's vineyard, and particularly for those on the cutting edge.

So we decided to order the equipment on faith.

It was a miracle that we even got financing for the buy. A year before, no creditor would look twice at us. Lending agencies were unimpressed by our vision. Giving by God's people improved so much in one year on the air that the same lending agencies now were eager to get involved. Amazing what a difference God's people can make in the world of big business. I am deeply and especially grateful to our friends who supported Channel 38 in that first year of touch-and-go.

After we ordered the equipment, we sent a letter out to our entire mailing list, explaining what we had done. We were asking the Lord, the letter said, for $50,000.

Then the staff joined in faith, believing that God would touch the hearts of our friends and partners as they received the letter.

Direct-mail experts will tell you that the most loyal mailing list returns only 20 percent on any giving project. In three weeks $54,425 came into our office. Glory to God!

But the studios we moved into would require more than just the basics. The basics would get us on the air, but they would not let us produce our own programs. Jim Bakker, president of the P.T.L. Network, invited Jerry and me to appear on the "P.T.L. Club," and during the program he announced that P.T.L. would supply the balance of our equipment needs—two color cameras, two videotape machines, and a time-base corrector. Since early on, the P.T.L. people have been generous and faithful friends of Channel 38, and I thank God for their continued support.

Our first day broadcasting from our new studios was Labor Day, September 5, 1977. We praised the Lord for allowing us a place of our own, with our own crews, our own equipment, our own schedule. It was a beautiful multiple blessing.

Since Channel 38 surfaced, dozens of people from all over the country have asked me, "How do you start a Christian television station?" Almost always they come bearing a list of conditions: if they get a certain amount of money or a certain number of names on their mailing list they will start.

But if Paul and Peter and even Jesus had operated their ministries according to their income and their popularity, all of Christianity would have come to a standstill 2,000 years ago!

I'm no expert. All I know is what I've learned by flunking God's tests. So all I dare to pass along is a single admonition: Start by determining God's will. If God has called you to anything—starting a Christian television station, opening a Christian coffeehouse, any imaginable ministry—then don't let anything keep you from seeing that vision through.

It is a paraphrase, perhaps, of my father's words of advice to me. "Starting but not stopping" became the ultimate rule of thumb for me. It is a simple principle, but treacherous to carry out in real life. Impossible, in fact—unless it's undergirded by faith. And that can only be implemented in a life by translating it into everyday discipline: large and equal amounts of prayer and God's Word.

This is the spark that inspired the dream.

Chapter 21

Dream at Our Fingertips

A woman lay helplessly in a hospital bed. The pain was so great she wanted to die. She watched TV, trying to get her mind off her agony.

Her world had fallen apart. Her husband had injured his back and had been out of work for eight months. They had five small children at home. Now, she could not walk.

At 7:30 p.m. she decided to dial once more around on the TV set and then try to get some sleep. Suddenly, she stopped dialing. A man on the screen was saying, "We can help you."

The woman was desperate. Then a phone number— 312/346-3800—lit up on the screen. She was intrigued.

"Could someone really help? Did someone really care?" she asked herself.

She risked it. A counselor answered. The two of them had a long, friendly talk. The counselor led her to trust Jesus Christ that night.

Within a month, filled with faith, the woman was suddenly and totally healed.

This story is repeated over and over. There are millions in Chicagoland just like her, hurting, needing.

They are in the swank Marina Towers, and in the gray steel-mill communities along the Lake, and in middle-class Griffith, Indiana. *Hurting*.

The signal goes out. The Word goes with it.

At some time or other, every person owning a television set in Chicagoland dials past Channel 38. We are there—helping the hurting, pointing the way to the Savior and Healer of mankind.

God loves the city. He has proved it undeniably. But He has determined to love it through us, His people.

It is an awesome responsibility, an awesome privilege, which God has entrusted to us. It is a weighty burden, a daily challenge, a fantastic dream. It is a dream of souls saved, a dream of lives transformed by the love of God.

The dream of Christian television in Chicagoland has not been fully realized. It is glimmering just beyond our fingertips. It will always be just beyond our reach, just outside the circle of our own will and power.

But no dream escapes faith. By faith we realize the dream, we accept the challenge, we shoulder the burden.

By faith we reach beyond our own circle and grasp the impossible.

"By faith Enoch was translated that he should not see death . . ."

By faith the vision of Channel 38 was born of foolishness, grew up facing the impossible, and yet refused to die.

"By faith Noah, being warned of God of things not seen as yet, moved with fear, prepared an ark to the saving of his house . . ."

By faith the vision of Channel 38 became more reality than dream, a set of future facts to be acted upon as if they had already occurred.

"By faith Abraham . . . obeyed; and he went out, not knowing whither he went."

By faith the vision of Channel 38, having nothing, followed God's course, God's timetable, God's mysterious plan.

"By faith Abraham, when he was tried, offered up Isaac..."

"By faith the vision of Channel 38 rose to the top of every stack, displacing all priorities, commanding every attention, toward the fulfilling of God's will.

"By faith they passed through the Red Sea as by dry land . . ."

By faith the vision of Channel 38 overcame financial crisis, emotional disaster, spiritual struggling—passed through every barrier, growing stronger with every test, growing brighter every day.

"By faith the walls of Jericho fell down . . ."

By faith the vision of Channel 38, having no power or wisdom of its own, beat all odds, changed the natural order of things, left the enemy staring gape-jawed—all to the glory of God, all to the accomplishing of God's will.

"And what shall I more say? for the time would fail me to tell of Gideon . . . and of Samson . . . of David also, and Samuel, and of the prophets; Who through faith subdued kingdoms, wrought righteousness, obtained promises, stopped the mouths of lions, quenched the violence of fire, escaped the edge of the sword, out of weakness were made strong. . ."

Here is a truth the Lord gave me many years ago. I don't know if it is original or not. So far as I know, it is, but we glean so much from others as we pass through life, that I cannot be sure.

"If I am what God wants me to be, He will teach me what He wants me to know, and help me do what He wants me to do."

The classic example of this in the Bible is Joseph. At the age of seventeen, he was suddenly ripped away from his home and his country. He would never again hear somebody pray to his Father's God. All the instruction in righteousness he would receive, he had already received.

If there was anyone who had a right to become bitter, it would be Joseph. Hated as a father's pet, envied by his brothers, misunderstood by his family, sold into slavery by his own flesh and blood, falsely accused by his master's wife, unjustly imprisoned by his master, forgotten by his fellow prisoner who could have spoken a good word for him, he was left to languish in the prison. The Bible says, "His feet were hurt in irons."

Yet, he kept his heart right with God. He was what God wanted him to be. When his master's wife tempted him to adultery, he said, "How then can I do this great wickedness, and sin against God?" (Genesis 39:9). When the two fellow

149

prisoners dreamed dreams that troubled them, Joseph said, "Do not interpretations belong to God?" (Genesis 40:8). When he was brought before Pharaoh to interpret his dreams, he said, "It is not in me: God shall give Pharaoh an answer of peace" (Genesis 41:16).

Egypt was a land of idolatry and immorality. It was an extremely rich land, excelling in culture. When Pharaoh "called for all the magicians of Egypt, and all the wise men thereof," he did not assemble an accumulation of ignorance. They knew things we do not know, such as how to embalm a body to remain intact for more than 4,000 years, and how to build pyramids without the aid of modern machinery like we know it.

Joseph had not enrolled at the University of Cairo, nor had he studied economics, political science, administration, organization, or promotion and publicity.

Yet the Pharaoh looked at all the wise men of Egypt and said to them, "Can we find such a one as this is, a man in whom the spirit of God is?" (Genesis 41:38). And he set him over all the affairs of the kingdom, saying "Only in the throne will I be greater than thou" (Genesis 41:40).

In the ensuing years, Joseph saved not only the land of Egypt, but his own people, and others from the surrounding nations.

He *was* what God wanted him to *be*, so God *taught* him what He wanted him to *know*, and *helped him do* what He wanted him to *do*.

The same principle is at work today.

The person who keeps his heart right with God, has an open channel through which he can receive God's knowledge, understanding and wisdom. Jesus said, "Blessed are the pure in heart: for they shall see God" (Matthew 5:8). This does not just mean that someday, out in the future, we shall see Him. But if our heart is pure, we can see God at work in our lives today.

When the managers of industry are looking for someone to perform a specific task, they try to find someone who has had the proper training, combined with the proper experience. God does not necessarily work that way.

In the world of professional religion, a certain amount of formal education is assumed to be necessary before a person can expect to receive an assignment. It was true in Jesus' day.

However, after the ascension, the Apostles started out to fulfill the great commission. Miracles began happening in their ministry. This greatly dismayed the religious leaders of their day. They observed these fishermen, and concluded they were only "ignorant and unlearned men."

However, upon further observation, they came to another conclusion, "They took knowledge of them that they had been with Jesus."

When Jesus called the disciples, the record says, "He ordained twelve that they should be with Him . . ." (Mark 3:14). But before He ordained them to preach, which immediately follows, He ordained them to "be with him."

This is the greatest qualification a person can have. If we take time to "be with him" He can impart to us any bit of knowledge He wants us to have. By being with Jesus, the disciples (Apostles) learned to preach and to perform miracles. Their critics could not "withstand the wisdom with which they spake."

"Ignorant and unlearned?" Yes. But Peter had walked with Jesus on the water, had gone with Him through Gethsemane, had accompanied Him to the cross—though falteringly—had examined the empty tomb, and had tarried in the upper room for Pentecost. His critics could not deny the evidence: the lame man stood before them whole. (Acts 4:14)

Jesus is wanting to do the same for you and me today. And will, if we meet the conditions.

An Afterword

My life is a composite of many others. This book is the product of many people. Channel 38 is the expression of God's love to Chicagoland poured through the channel of many lives. These pages stand as a tribute to some of those, without whom Channel 38, this book, and my own life would not be possible.

This volume is lovingly dedicated to:

My father, Claud Clarence Carr, who by his example taught me the importance of faithfulness in church attendance, the necessity of daily devotions, the pattern of generosity, and the principle of hard work.

My mother, Alvina Louise (Thorman) Carr, whose consistent life became a manifestation of the love of God to me, whose discipline was always administered in love; who not only spent many hours reading the Scriptures to me in my early childhood, but taught me to commit God's Word to memory.

To Priscilla Faye (Seidner) Carr, my faithful wife, who took seriously the vows "for better, for worse, for richer, for poorer, in sickness and in health," and who has provided love, inspiration, and balance for my life.

To David and Marilyn, our two children, who always thought I was more than I am, and by whose expectation I was prodded to become something I wasn't.

To the Reverend Victor Georg Greisen, my first district superintendent (or "Bishop"), who became my ideal for the ministry, setting an example of godliness, prayer, and indomitable faith; who challenged me to attempt things beyond my ability and never to take "no" for an answer.

To The Stone Church, 6330 West 127th Street, Palos Heights, Illinois, a congregation whose members gave generously of their money and unselfishly of their time, who spent days in prayer and work, and who encouraged their pastor to pursue a dream until it became reality.

To The Stone Church board, who shared the excitement of an impossible vision and said, "Pastor, God has laid this vision on your heart. Take whatever time is necessary to see it fulfilled. Let your staff do your work, but pursue the vision God has given you."

To Taylor H. Davis, assistant pastor, who carried much of my pastoral responsibilities, so I could devote many months to a project which had little chance of success. Without his support the project might not have succeeded.

To Martin Ozinga, Jr., and the First National Bank of Evergreen Park, Illinois, who exhibited unusual faith in making a loan for $600,000. In retrospect, I can think of many reasons why he should never have done this, and few reasons why he should have. But, following an impulse of the Holy Spirit, this bank became a partner in God's expression of love to Chicagoland.

To Elaine Wilson, my efficient, dedicated, and hardworking secretary, by whose consistent promptings a vast amount of this material was dictated, working literally day and night, she is the one person—more than any other—who is responsible for this book now being in print.

To Doug Brendel, the talented young writer, who took the hundreds of pages of rough manuscript and transformed them into the volume you hold in your hand.

To Robert Walker, editor of *Christian Life* magazine and president of Creation House, who guided us through the wilderness of our uncertainty, in a field about which we knew nothing, to help us publish our first book.

To the dedicated members of our staff, who have provided unusual backing and strength, without whom the ministry of Channel 38 would grind to a halt.

To the thousands of people who pray and give, without whom there would be no ministry at all on Channel 38. It is you, the reader of this book, an instrument in God's hands, who perpetuates the ministry God brought into being. Your prayers sustain us, your gifts support us, and together we can Win Chicagoland For Christ.

Owen C. Carr
Chicago, Illinois